The Chicago Trunk Murder

NORTHERN

ILLINOIS

UNIVERSITY

PRESS

DeKalb

The
Chicago
Trunk Murder

Law and Justice at the Turn of the Century

ELIZABETH DALE

© 2011 by Northern Illinois University Press

Published by the Northern Illinois University Press, DeKalb, Illinois 60115

Manufactured in the United States using acid-free paper.

All Rights Reserved

Design by Julia Fauci

Library of Congress Cataloging-in-Publication Data

Dale, Elizabeth.

The Chicago trunk murder / Elizabeth Dale.

   p.   cm.

Includes bibliographical references and index.

ISBN 978-0-87580-440-8 (cloth: alk. paper)

1. Murder—Illinois—Chicago—Case studies. 2. Discrimination in criminal justice

administration—Illinois—Chicago—Case studies. 3. Immigrants—Illinois—Chicago—

History—19th century. 4. Italians—Illinois—Chicago—History—19th century. 5. Chicago

(Ill.)—History—19th century. I. Title.

HV6534.C4D35 2011

364.152′3092277311—dc22

2011011454

Contents

Illustrations

Acknowledgments

• Historians who work in one place and write about people and events in another build up a mountain of debts quickly. In this case, I am obliged to people in several cities and towns. Many of my colleagues at the University of Florida and at other institutions provided pointers or information or otherwise helped me with a variety of things from nineteenth-century Italian to the mysteries of forensic science. In particular, I thank Jeff Adler, Joel Black, Scott Catey, Steven Drizin, H. Roger Grant, Tom Green, Valerie Hans, Howard Louthan, Christopher Slobogin, Joseph Spillane, Andrea Sterk, and Luise White. I also want to thank my colleagues at the Levin College of Law at the University of Florida, who heard a very early version of part of this book in an enrichment seminar and made helpful comments.

My work on the Pittsburgh side of things was helped along the way by the people at the Allegheny County Medical Examiners' Office and reference librarians at Carnegie Mellon University and the University of Pittsburgh. My efforts to track down people and places in Chicago would not have been possible without the help I received from the interlibrary loan staff at the University of Florida. I also appreciate the assistance of Chris Winters from the Map Collection of the Joseph Regenstein Library at the University of Chicago. Other librarians and archivists helped enormously as well, especially the reference librarians at the Joseph Regenstein Library at the University of Chicago and the archivists at the Newberry Library and the Chicago History Museum, as well as the friendly people at the Attorney Registration and Disciplinary Committee for Illinois and Calvary Catholic Cemetery in Chicago and the archivists at the Secretary of State's Office for the State of Illinois (who copied files and helped me find things) and the archives staff at the Office of the Clerk of the Circuit Court of Cook County.

In trying to find out about the lawyers in the case I was assisted by the librarians at Howard University Law School and alumni offices at Brown University and the University of Michigan Law School. In addition, I appreciate the fact that my father, Charles Dale, spent the better part of an entire day sitting in the stacks of a library poring over the *Lakeside Directory* to track down jurors for me. Finally, because this turn-of-the-century project was researched at the turn of another century, I benefited from two online resources as well. The Church of the Latter Day Saints (LDS) has put vast amounts of genealogical material online, including passenger lists, census data, and vital statistics material for many other countries (including Italy). I used their materials to find out as much as I could about the defendants and other people who appeared in this case. Likewise, the descendents of the immigrants from Termini Imerese have created their own genealogical website, which includes English language translations of many of the materials filmed by the LDS.

The portion of the Chicago map printed in this book—"Index Map of Chicago: Running South to Seventy First Street" (Chicago: Rufus Blanchard, 1888)—was provided by the Map Collection at the Joseph Regenstein Library at the University of Chicago. It is available online at www.lib.uchicago.edu/e/su/maps/chifire/G4104-C6-1888-B53.html. And part of the material in the Introduction was published in my essay "It Makes Nothing Happen: Reasons for Studying the History of Law," *Law, Culture and the Humanities* 5 (2009), and is used here with permission.

A Note on Names

• Determining the proper spelling of people's names was a problem of massive proportions in this case. News accounts had a hard time with nearly everyone's name, not just those of the Italian defendants. For the purpose of coherence, I have standardized spellings of names throughout the text, although I have kept the original—and often wildly disparate—spellings in the newspaper headlines in the notes. In the case of the parties, I adopted the spelling in the court records, even though those records garbled several of the defendants' names. In other instances, I have tried to use the spelling of names set out in the *Lakeside Annual Business Directory of the City of Chicago, 1885* (Chicago: Donnelly, Gassette & Lloyd, 1885) wherever possible. When all else failed, I simply picked one of the various spellings.

The case of Pittsburgh, which was also subject to the vagaries of late nineteenth-century spelling, deserves a special note all its own. At the time of this case, although some people already used the now common spelling "Pittsburgh," the prevailing spelling was "Pittsburg," without a final "h." Throughout this study I have followed the example of the *Pittsburg Dispatch* and omitted the "h."

The Chicago Trunk Murder

Introduction   Rule of Justice or Rule of Law?

•   In 1885 five Italian immigrants went on trial in Chicago accused of murdering a fellow émigré, stuffing his body into a trunk, and
shipping it to Pittsburg. At the end of the case the jury found three of
the men guilty of murder and acquitted the two others. Less than four
months later, the three found guilty were hanged. It was a fascinating
crime that turned into a spectacular trial; from the discovery of the
body through to the guilty verdict, the Trunk Murder case received
extensive coverage in Chicago's newspapers and the attention of press
around the country.[1]
One hundred years later, I began practicing law in a small civil rights
firm in Chicago. It was a frustrating time for Chicago's civil rights
bar; the federal courts had begun to change and we watched as the
law our clients depended on disappeared, often as a result of cases we
had brought. As appeals to economic reasoning began to supplant
sociological jurisprudence at the Seventh Circuit, I convinced myself
that we needed our own perspective on constitutional law, a theory that
would help us push back against the paradigm shift. Because theories
of original intent were in the air, I turned to history, modestly assuming
that if I studied constitutional history carefully enough I could either
bend originalism to my will or refute it. And either way, I reasoned,
I would probably find a historical narrative that would reinforce our
legal arguments. So I began to spend my spare time reading constitutional and legal history. Working as methodically as I could, I read
my way through all the constitutional histories I could find, and when

I could not find more books on the subject, I turned to books on legal history. Once I got to the point where I could no longer find any more books with the words "law" and "history" in the title, I began to read other types of history, including histories of the late eighteenth and early nineteenth centuries, books about the Civil War and slavery, and works on Reconstruction. Then, after I had read all this, I decided to abandon my scheme.[2]

My reading did confirm my suspicion that much of the constitutional law I knew rested on naïve, even distorted, views of the past. At the same time, my reading made it clear that there was no grand narrative of constitutional history out there waiting to be uncovered by a clever, if increasingly bleary-eyed, young lawyer. In fact, my reading called into question the whole idea of looking for a single story of constitutional history. Most of the works I read seemed bound and determined to resist being made part of a single narrative. They did not build on each other; frequently they did not even respond to, or cite, one another. The histories I read were products of legal history's law and society turn and, as a result, usually did embed their discussions of law into larger social contexts. But even they treated legal issues and periods of time in isolation rather than as parts of some grand historical design—and the nonlegal histories were even more amazing, at least to someone whose day job involved the practice of law. More often than not, those studies ignored the role of law and legal issues entirely, as if courts and lawyers, judges and clients (to say nothing of property rights, contract claims, tort actions, or criminal prosecutions) had no impact on the workings of the world they described. The historians' resistance to even a hint of a grand narrative of U.S. history was so absolute it would have been splendid if I had been in the mood to admire it. But I was feeling too beleaguered to marvel. Instead I threw up my hands, sure that there was nothing practical to be gained from historical study.

Then, as the 1980s came to an end and the state of civil rights practice in Chicago grew so precarious that it was clear I would need to look for something else to do, I decided the reasonable thing was to go to graduate school to study the history of law. This time, my intentions were different. I did not hope to find the grand, alternative narrative I had been unable to locate during my studies after work. Instead, I went to graduate school because I had decided: history that emphasized multiple, particularized, narratives actually was worth doing. This shift reflected a change in my understanding of the audience for legal history. When I had hoped to come up with a grand, new constitutional narrative, my assumption was that its audience would consist of judges, lawyers, and law professors. But at some point it dawned on me that there were other people with a stake in law and the legal system—future litigants, potential jurors, voters, and the public at large, people who felt that they had been barred from understanding the mysterious workings of law. So I went to graduate school with those people in mind. In effect, though I did not put it in these terms in 1990, I wanted to use legal and constitutional history as a way of promoting popular constitutionalism—as a way of giving the law, with its complicated past and ambiguous future, back to the people.

One way to do this was to teach legal and constitutional history outside of law schools, to students who would not become lawyers. This would help people outside the law get a feel for how it worked and perhaps a sense that they could understand what courts did. Another way was to teach constitutional and legal history to law students, to help them see the context of the cases they read in class and to put back into the cases those poor widows and orphans their contracts professors had taught them to ignore. Neither course would offer students a single better way of understanding law or the constitution; either would let the students see they could understand law and the constitution as something other than a set of rules or the practices of a courtroom. And this, I hoped, might inspire some of them to become more engaged observers of the legal system, the courts, and constitutional debates. A final way to help bring law back to the people was to write histories of particular legal moments, of cases and appeals, to help make the unfamiliar workings of the world of law more familiar, while showing how contingent the processes of law could be. Cases, after all, were events that were inevitably interpreted and reinterpreted and then reinterpreted again: Parties and witnesses crafted narratives to describe injuries or legal needs, lawyers interpreted those narratives into specific legal frameworks and then, if there was a trial, reinterpreted those legal frameworks into more popular narratives of justice or desert. Judges hearing the case provided further interpretations, as did news reports or other popular accounts. Much later, other cases might revisit those interpretations and modify them yet again. Those interpretations and their interaction are a fundamental aspect of law, an aspect that took it out of the world of system and grand narratives and revealed it for the particularized, contingent, and multilayered thing it was.

Nearly ten years after I finished graduate school, Robert Darnton gave that kind of history a name when he published an essay in the *New York Review of Books* about a style of history he called "incident analysis." As the name suggests, this analysis is the study of particular, usually brief, incidents: trials, riots, strikes, and battles. It tries to re-construct events as completely as the evidence allows but also explores the way an event was interpreted and reinterpreted both at the time and by those who learned about the event long after it happened. In Darnton's words, incident analysis "deals with the concatenation of events rather than merely the events themselves. It attempts to find their meanings—what they meant to the people who experienced them and to those who learned about them later. It therefore concentrates on reports of incidents and the way they echoed through various modes of communications."[3]

And so this book is an incident analysis. It looks at Chicago's Trunk Murder and the stories that were subsequently told about it; first by the police as they investigated the crime, then by the court system as the case was tried, and by the newspapers throughout the period that covered both the investigation and the trial. This book traces out the investigation of the crime, the false starts, the missed opportunities, and the leaps in logic that led to the arrest of five recent Italian immigrants for murder. Then it follows their confused path through the legal system, a path that ended when two of the men were acquitted and the other three convicted and sentenced to die. In this respect it is a history of the history, or histories, of a crime and its punishment.

At the same time, like any incident analysis, this is a study of a trial that took place at a particular place and time, and the way in which that context influenced the outcome of this trial. Because the defen-dants in this case were immigrants one might guess that context would boil down to a single question: How well did Chicago's felony court system work for the city's immigrant population? That was certainly something that people worried about in turn-of-the-century Chicago. The percentage of foreign-born people in the U.S. population went from just over 10 percent in 1880 to 14.7 percent in 1910, and in many urban areas the numbers were much higher. In 1880 Chicago had a total population of just over 500,000 and roughly half that number was foreign born or had foreign-born parents. By 1890 the city had more than doubled in size and 79 percent of its 1.1 million residents had been born in other countries or were the children of immigrants. By 1910 Chicago's population had grown to almost 2.2 million, and not quite half (900,000) of those residents were immigrants or their chil-dren. These numbers meant that many people, in Chicago and in other parts of the United States, worried about how immigrants were treated by the courts and the law.[4]

At first glance, the Trunk Murder case suggests that those who worried about the treatment of immigrants in Chicago's criminal courts were right to do so. It is clear that the defendants in the Trunk Murder case did not get a fair trial, and this surely confirms the suspicion voiced by the *Chicago Times* in November 1885—their trial was unfair because they were immigrants. Yet other evidence from turn-of-the-century Chicago suggests the problem was more complex. Jeffrey Adler's research on homicides in Chicago between 1875 and 1920 established that Italians had the highest murder rate in the city. But he also found that, across the fifty-five-year period covered by his study, only 24 percent of the city's murders resulted in a conviction and that immigrant groups, including Italians, were convicted at the same low rate.[5]

Adler determined that most defendants found guilty of homicide in Chicago were sentenced very leniently and discovered that the treatment of Italian immigrants conformed to this general rule. The treatment of the few Italians brought to trial for murder in Chicago before the Trunk Murder case was consistent with his findings. The first Italian charged with murder in Chicago was Francesco Borrono, who was charged with murdering another Italian, Godzordo Genoraway, in September 1874, but Borrono was never brought to trial. In 1878 L. P. Simoni (or Sominski), an Italian ragpicker, was arrested for shooting Nick McCue during a quarrel over some trash. Simoni was charged with murder, but like Borrono he was never tried. Instead he took a course that became increasingly popular with criminal defendants in the late nineteenth century and pled guilty in exchange for a sentence of fourteen years in prison. The first Italian actually to be tried for murder in Chicago was a woman, Teresa Sturla, who was brought to trial in 1882 for murdering her lover, Charles Stiles. Their relationship had been a tempestuous one, and after a particularly ugly quarrel Sturla went to Stiles's room in Chicago's Palmer House Hotel and shot him. Stiles died; Sturla quickly confessed and was charged. At her trial, Sturla argued that she was temporarily insane when she killed Stiles, rendered mad by his beatings and abuse. While it is not clear that the jury accepted her claim of insanity, they clearly were ambivalent about her crime. Ultimately, they found her guilty but sentenced her to only one year in jail. Three cases involving Italian immigrants, one that never went to trial, one that ended with a plea, and a third that resulted in a conviction and a very light sentence. Most of Chicago's murders were resolved in very similar ways, with the result that the few homicide suspects found guilty of murder were sentenced very leniently. But this was not what happened in the Trunk Murder case. And so the question, again, is why? In the end, in this study I argue that the answer to this question turns as much on the relation of law to justice as it does on the fact that the defendants in this case were immigrants.[6]

To trace out that point, this book builds on a number of recent studies that have sketched the historical tension between "rough justice," the violent acts of lynch mobs and vigilante groups, and "due process," the rules and procedures that made up the criminal justice system in the United States. Those works have traced the roots of rough justice back to Anglo-American legal cultural assumptions that vested the power to judge and punish in local communities, matched punishment to offense, and favored swift retribution over deliberation. In the early years of the Republic, the older traditions prevailed and meant that local communities controlled the courts and were able to see that the criminal justice system reflected community norms. In that period, law and justice were often, but not entirely, the same. By the Civil War, when law had become more doctrinal and courts were increasingly less responsive to community will, justice and law began to occupy two separate realms. Law, defined by neutrality and precedent, had begun to favor the principles of due process over retribution, and so, popular justice moved out of the courts and took on an extralegal form. For the next seventy years, proponents of due process struggled to bring rough justice under control, arguing that the government should have the monopoly on judging and punishing wrongdoers. Ultimately, by the 1930s, advocates of due process had largely won and had managed to cast rough justice as uncivilized and insufficiently modern. As the historian Michael Pfeifer has shown, the history of this triumph is a story of compromise. Due process prevailed in the 1930s because its proponents embraced the death penalty, bringing a crucial element of rough justice—the element of retribution—into the courts.[7]

In this study I look at a slightly earlier period, exploring how, at the turn of the century, the criminal justice system intersected with popular justice. In an earlier study, *Rule of Justice,* I looked at a single trial to see how popular forces could put pressure on the criminal justice system, from the police to the courts. In this book I also explore that interplay, though I am looking at the relationship between popular justice and formal law from a slightly different perspective. While in the first book I emphasized the extent to which extralegal forces could influence the criminal justice system and help determine a verdict, here the question is how popular forces were brought into the criminal justice system.

I show how closely the press participated in police investigations, allowing the people a vicarious role in exposing the wrongdoers, and consider the results of this involvement. Sometimes the police used the press, but more often than not the press used the police, pushing them to ignore those rules, some as old and well established as habeas corpus and some constitutionally mandated, that interfered with the prompt resolution of the case. At the same time, I study the ways in which the idea of justice was insinuated into trials, through the principle that commonsense notions of justice were superior to the demands of legal rules and the determination of the jury more important than adherence to law. By unpacking this dynamic, in this history of the Trunk Murder trial, we refine our understanding of how the transformation from rough justice to due process occurred. By the end of this process, rough justice may have been co-opted by due process so that only the death penalty remained, but along the way to that transformation, popular forces played a bigger role, pressing the legal system from the outside and working within it to co-opt its principles as well.[8]

Chapter One

An Italian Murder

• The trunk caused problems from the moment baggage agents at Pittsburg's Union Depot carried it off the Pittsburg, Ft. Wayne & Chicago Express just after 6:00 a.m. on Friday, May 1, 1885. In most respects it was unremarkable. New, shiny, cheap, the imitation steamer trunk was roughly twenty inches deep, about as wide, and not quite three and a half feet long. It was edged with strips of sheet metal painted black and covered by some yellow paper striped with brown paint to resemble wood panels. There were other strips of painted metal tacked at intervals around its sides; its lid was latched on with hasps and those fittings were reinforced by a cord lashed around it. The shipping label on its side carried the straightforward direction "from Chicago to Pittsburg, P.R.R. No. 4171."[1]

But it stank.

By mid-morning the smell was so bad that the baggage agents at the station moved the trunk out of the luggage room and onto the platform. By late afternoon even that was not enough, so when no one had come to claim the trunk by 5:00 p.m., C. S. Jenkins, the baggage master at the station, determined to investigate. After first tipping the trunk on its side, which made its contents slide from one end to the other, he untied the rope that bound the top down and pried open the lid.[2]

Inside was the decomposing body of a man. When he was alive he had been about 5 foot 6 inches tall and weighed between 150 and 160 pounds. What was left of him now was doubled over and lying on the side, trussed with a cord that bound his arms and legs together in front of his body and had been knotted securely around his neck. Blood, vomit, or something else flecked his smooth-shaven face, which, like the rest of his body, was very swollen. His tongue stuck out of his gaping mouth and his face was so black that, as one newspaper put it, "they thought at first he was a colored man." A quick search of the dead man's pockets disclosed nothing more than a receipt for a money order that had been sent to Filippo Caruso, Termini Imerese, Sicily, in February 1885 and a Chicago streetcar ticket.[3]

With this discovery, things moved quickly. Jenkins sent word of the body to the Alleghany County coroner, Peter Dressler. Someone contacted the press. Meanwhile two doctors for the railroad, William Hamilton and Charles Shaw, were called in to examine the body and, because Dressler was not a doctor, perform the autopsy. Hamilton and Shaw quickly determined that rigor mortis had ended completely by the time the body was discovered, which suggested the man in the trunk had been dead at least thirty-six hours. The two also found the lungs of the corpse were engorged with blood and observed that there were "no marks of extravasation [sic] of the blood in the tissues of his neck, or laceration of the muscles [in the neck] observed, or laceration of the windpipe." At something of a loss to explain the precise cause of death given this evidence, Hamilton and Shaw initially suggested that the man in the trunk could still have met his death by strangling, noting that it was possible that "strangulation might have taken place without leaving marks of injury on the neck."[4]

Not long after the autopsy was completed, the coroner convened an inquest over the body. According to a lengthy report in the *Pittsburg Dispatch*, Hamilton told the coroner's jury that his examination suggested the body in the trunk had been dead several days, though probably not more than three. Shaw and Hamilton added that the evidence suggested the death was a homicide, although they continued to equivocate about how the man died, telling the coroner's jury that there were several possibilities: The victim might have been strangled and died before he was put in the trunk; he might have been put into the trunk alive only to die later of suffocation or because he strangled himself as he struggled against the rope wrapped around his neck. After deliberating briefly, the jury returned a verdict that declared that "an unknown man between 25 and 30 years of age was found dead in a trunk May 1, 1885, which arrived on train number 8 that left Chicago at 3:15 p.m. April 30, 1885, and arrived at Union depot at 6:10 a.m., May 1, 1885, and from all of the evidence taken we, the jury, find that he died from strangulation, committed by some person or persons unknown to the jury."[5]

First Clues

The next morning stories in newspapers around the country told their readers about the remarkable crime. In Pittsburg hundreds of people, mostly Italian, went to Flannery's Undertakers to see if they recognized the man from the trunk. At least two of the visitors, Mrs. Bonistalli and Antonio Sabino, identified the body as Bonistalli's brother Pietro Caruso, a peanut vender who had lived in Pittsburg for several years before moving to Chicago to work on the railroad. But the Pittsburg police department decided not to credit this identification and made arrangements to have the body buried in an unmarked grave the next day.[6]

Meanwhile, other details began to emerge. A story in the *St. Louis Globe-Democrat* reported that S. M. Jackson, an expressman who loaded the trunk onto the train in Chicago, recalled noticing the trunk smelled even then. Jackson added that he suspected at the time that the trunk contained a dead body. A Chicago paper carried the news that Samuel Coyle, one of the baggage agents in Pittsburg, claimed he saw a suspicious-looking man in the vicinity of the trunk when it arrived at the Pittsburg station. Coyle was quoted as recalling that the man looked like an "Irish raftsman," was about 5 foot 5 or 6 inches tall, had a "dark, short mustache," and wore "a long, rough gray overcoat" with a "large slouch hat of the western style." Coyle reported that the mysterious raftsman followed the trunk off the train and into the baggage room, gazed around for a few minutes and then left.[7]

In those first days after the discovery of the body, the basic details of the case changed at breakneck speed and reports in the various papers were often inconsistent or contradictory. According to initial accounts in the *Chicago Tribune* no one from the baggage room in Chicago could remember anyone who brought in a trunk to be shipped to Pittsburg on April 30, but just a day later, the *Tribune* reported that a baggage handler named J. O'Brien remembered that two Italians had checked a trunk in around 11:00 a.m. on April 30. In contrast, the *St. Louis Globe-Democrat* and the *Chicago Herald* reported that the baggage handler was sure that three Italians dropped the trunk off, while the story of the discovery in the *Pittsburg Dispatch* avoided precision entirely and simply indicated that the baggage men in Chicago recalled that trunk number 4147 was checked by a "party of Italians." A few days later, the *Tribune* changed its report again, joining the consensus that set the number of men who dropped the trunk off at the station at three.[8]

A *Padrone*

At least everyone could agree that the victim was an Italian, and this conclusion quickly shaped accounts of the crime. Chicago's police officers spread out to trace the money order found in the dead man's pocket. In a blow to department pride it took an amateur detective, the Italian saloonkeeper and special policeman Emilio DeStefano, to find the carbon of the money order at a local post office branch. Fortunately, that carbon provided what seemed to be an important detail, revealing that the money order had been purchased by a man who listed his address as 267 Milwaukee Avenue, Chicago, which turned out to be the address of a fruit and candy store managed by Joseph Poli. So the police promptly arrested Poli and the eleven or so Italian men who lived in the basement under his shop.[9]

Not long after this, the police arrested Andrea Russo, the owner of the store on Milwaukee Avenue. Russo promptly became the focus of the investigation. One Chicago paper called attention to the fact that Russo, whom it described as a "small, poorly dressed, light complexioned Italian, with cunning and restless eyes," closely resembled the description of the man who took the trunk to the station in Chicago to ship it to Pittsburg. There was a slight setback when the baggage handler who said he checked the trunk at Chicago could not identify Russo or any of the other Italians in custody. Undeterred, the Chicago police refused to release any of the Italians they had arrested, though police captain John Bonfield, who was running the investigation out of Chicago's Desplaines Avenue police station, conceded that most of the men would have to be released the next day unless someone was able to identify at least one of them. Bonfield assured the citizens of Chicago that Andrea Russo would remain in custody even if he was not identified. In part, Russo was suspect because he had given inconsistent statements to the police. Initially he denied that he knew anyone named Caruso and then changed his story when confronted with the evidence that Russo had purchased the money order for Caruso in February.[10]

Yet as far as the local papers were concerned, Russo was not just suspicious because he was a liar; he was a suspect because he was a *padrone. Padroni* became anathema in the United States and Europe in the 1870s following troubling reports of Italian "bosses" who tricked children into a type of slavery. The bosses entered into contracts of indenture, either with the children themselves or with their parents or guardians, promising to take the children to a city in Europe or the

United States where they would be taught a trade. In practice what seemed to happen all too often was that the children, usually boys in their mid teens, were taken to another country where they were sent out into city streets. There they played music or begged for money, which they then had to turn over to their padrone.[11]

This exploitation of children by padroni became a scandal in New York and several other U.S. cities. At one trial a New York City police officer estimated that between two and three thousand children were enslaved to padroni in that city alone. Some stories recounted efforts to pursue padroni through the criminal justice system; others reported that communities refused to wait for the law and dealt with the problem themselves. When a suspected padrone appeared in Little Rock, Arkansas, with fourteen boys in tow, his troop was met by a delegation from the local Italian community. They seized the boys, who were taken in by Italian families, and drove the padrone out of town.[12]

Italians were not the only children exploited by padroni, but a vigorous campaign prompted the Italian government to take an active role in trying to crush the practice. It passed a law in 1873 intended to prevent padroni from taking unrelated children to the United States for money. In 1874 the United States passed a complementary law designed to restrict the immigration of children traveling without their parents. Organizations like the Society for Prevention of Cruelty to Children, the Society for Lost, Stolen or Abused Children, and the Charity Organization Society in New York sprang up and worked to end the padroni system, offering sanctuary for children trying to escape their servitude or suing to get children out of their contracts with padroni.[13]

Generally, these efforts worked. By the 1880s denunciations of padroni had shifted focus from the exploitation of children to a new problem: padroni had begun to meet adult immigrants as they came into the city, "prevail[ing] on them to sign a pretended contract, securing their services for a year, two years, or longer, as the case may be, at a certain remuneration." To secure their loyalty and prevent them from seeking help from other sources, the unscrupulous padroni warned their marks that Americans hated Italians. Once again, governments tried to intervene. In 1885, the United States passed the Foran Act, which made it illegal "for any person, company, partnership, or corporation, in any manner whatsoever to prepay the transportation, or in any way assist or encourage the importation or migration of any alien or aliens, any foreigner or foreigners, into the United States . . . under contract or agreement . . . to perform labor or services of any kind in the United States." The Italian government established a labor bureau at Ellis Island in the 1890s, in the hopes that it would prevent Italian immigrants from coming under a padroni's control. A few years later, the Italian government created a labor referral center in New York City for the same purpose.[14]

But in contrast to the efforts to keep padroni from exploiting children, attempts to protect adult émigrés were not particularly successful. Padroni interacted with adult immigrants at too many levels to be easily stopped, they loaned money to help immigrants travel and then loaned them more money once they landed. Russo was apparently guilty of all these things; he advanced money to help men emigrate from Sicily, loaned them more money to set up as peddlers, and then supplied them with the goods that they sold from their carts. The presence of the dozen or so men living at the candy shop on Milwaukee Avenue suggested that he also offered his peddlers shelter, presumably in exchange for rent or service.[15]

Today historians disagree about whether padroni aided or exploited their clients. Some argue that the padrone virtually enslaved those he aided by burdening them with debt, while others argue that padroni provided useful services for immigrants who otherwise had little access to housing, employment contacts, or sources of credit. In May 1885 the *Chicago Tribune* knew no doubt. Its columns cast Russo as an Italian "boss," a "money-lender with Shylock proclivities," and a man known in his neighborhood as "the murderer."[16]

And a Peddler

So, two days after the discovery of the body in the trunk, a working theory of the case had already emerged. The police hypothesized that Russo was a padrone who killed Caruso in the course of some sort of financial dispute. Confirmation for this theory seemed to come, in the form of yet another Italian immigrant, on Sunday, May 3. That afternoon a man appeared at Chicago's Desplaines Avenue police station. He proclaimed that he was Francesco Caruso and he was sure the man in the trunk was his brother, Filippo. Francesco was accompanied by Lorenz Ryder, who owned a candy shop on Rebecca Street and told police he was the Caruso brothers' landlord. The two told an ominous tale.[17]

Speaking through Ryder, who translated for him, Francesco Caruso explained that his brother Filippo was a fruit peddler from Termini Imerese, Sicily. Sometime around 9:00 a.m. on Thursday, April 30, Filippo left their apartment on Tilden Avenue to go and look for a new peddling route. According to Francesco, when he left that morning his brother was carrying "$350 in gold and greenbacks hidden inside his waistcoat." As important, Francesco also assured the police that Andrea Russo was a longtime acquaintance, who had known both Caruso brothers when they lived in Termini Imerese and had done business with them both when they moved to Chicago.[18]

Francesco Caruso's story certainly seemed to confirm the basic details of the police theory, and by establishing that Filippo Caruso was a fruit peddler Francesco added another twist to the case. While padroni were invariably cast as villains, Italian street peddlers occupied a more ambiguous place in the popular imagination. Mostly immigrants, peddlers were not as respectable as salesmen. Typically native born, salesmen worked for specific dealers and filled previously made orders, which they sometimes supplemented with impromptu sales to regular customers. In contrast, Chicago's immigrant peddlers existed at the margins of the economy and the law. Their arrangements with the stores or dealers from whom they bought the goods they sold were often informal and they plied their trade throughout the city. Some peddlers staked a claim to a specific spot, others traveled back and forth along a particular route.[19]

There were some immigrant shopkeepers, like Lorenz Ryder and Andrea Russo, who worked with peddlers, but many of Chicago's merchants battled peddlers as ferociously as governments fought the padroni. Shopkeepers objected to the competition from peddlers who parked themselves right outside their shop doors, making sales to potential customers. They also resented the itinerant peddlers, who gave customers a reason to avoid going out to stores. And because peddlers sold everything from beer to fruit, bread, butter, candy, popcorn, tinware, and books, they competed with many different types of businesses. Shopkeepers were the loudest in their objections, but they were not alone. Customers, the police, and newspapers also complained that peddlers sold bad, rotten, or otherwise adulterated goods. Beer peddlers were accused of selling liquor to minors; peddlers in business and residential areas were suspected of using their peddling to gain entrance into the places they later burglarized. Other peddlers, like the padroni, appeared to exploit children: people complained about seeing children, sometimes girls as young as eight, selling apples for peddlers on Chicago's streets.[20]

State and local governments had long licensed peddlers in the effort to control them, and Chicago was no exception, though its efforts were neither consistent nor effective. In 1880 the Chicago Citizens' Association, a group dedicated to law and order, declared that unlicensed peddlers were a public nuisance that had only "to some extent" abated. Responding to pressure from the association, shopkeepers, and the *Chicago Tribune,* Chicago police began to target curbside fruit peddlers in the early 1880s. Their efforts were complicated by the city council. In 1882 the council raised the licensing fee for peddlers and hawkers to $10 a year; then, just over a month later, the council lowered the rate to $5, only to raise the price of the peddlers' license back up to $10 the next year. The council's dithering was doubtless frustrating to the police and the citizens' association, but it was also largely irrelevant. Peddlers could, and did, easily evade the licensing fee. Some simply ignored the requirement; others sold their wares on the strip of land in front of the federal courthouse, which was not subject to Chicago ordinances because it was considered federal land.[21]

Although citizens' groups, grocers, and governments often cast peddlers as noisy, annoying, and dishonest elements of city life, customers were more than ready to buy peddlers' wares. And newspapers, even the censorious *Chicago Tribune,* undermined their own attacks on street peddlers by celebrating the color that peddlers added to Chicago's streets. A steady stream of articles described the exotic things that peddlers sold or recounted tales of peddlers who came to the aid of others by thwarting crimes or by matchmaking for shy customers. Other stories reminded their readers that peddlers were often victims, struggling against interlopers who tried to steal their routes or undersell them. Not all peddlers were the passive economic marks these stories described, of course, but even the most economically savvy peddler was vulnerable to other threats, and a steady stream of news accounts made clear that the men with their carts and trays were often the subject of petty harassment, outright theft, and physical attack.[22]

If Filippo Caruso was a peddler, this made him a sympathetic foil for the padrone Andrea Russo, and news accounts began to portray him as a frugal young entrepreneur. But a careful reader of these stories might wonder about the portrait Francesco provided of his brother. The body in the trunk had been well-dressed: several news accounts spoke of silk underclothes and a new pair of Congress gaiters, a soft-sided shoe. Silk underclothes were hardly cheap, and Congress gaiters were the pricey shoes of an office worker, not the sturdy, cheap boots of a man who spent his days walking the city's streets hawking oranges. More puzzling was Francesco's claim about his brother's hefty bank roll. The fact that Filippo had extra cash appeared to be true; other Italians in Chicago told reporters that Filippo Caruso liked to flash his money, counting it while he stood in a window, and keeping it in a big roll that he often tossed in the air. But while it seemed incontestable that Filippo Caruso had a lot of money, it was unclear how a fruit peddler could have acquired so much cash.[23]

Lawless Sicilians?

The next step was clear. Francesco Caruso was packed off to Pittsburg along with detective James Bonfield, Captain John Bonfield's brother, to identify the body, but in other respects, the investigation into the murder seemed to grind to a halt. Police officers trying to trace the trunk and its journey to the train station's baggage room on April 30 met with little success, causing one newspaper to speculate that either the trunk salesman wanted to keep his identity hidden or that the trunk had been purchased by a third party to "baffle inquiry." The police had a much simpler explanation, as one of the detectives working on the case put it: "Talk about Chinamen—I'd rather work up ten Chinese cases than one 'dago.' The lower class of Italians seem to be leagued together under some sort of tacit agreement never to give each other away under penalty of death. They have a habit of marking a man who 'squeals' to the police. The result is that nothing will get them to talk if they don't want to. And then the multiplicity of their dialects furnishes an easy refuge from cross-examination."[24]

Those complaints about clannish Italians who meted out their own rough justice rather than rely on the institutions of the law evoke the image of *omertà* offered by modern studies of the Mob, but the reality in 1885 was much less dramatic and far more complex. Even in 1885 the mafia was not unknown to popular culture; a few years earlier *Lippincott's Magazine of Popular Literature* carried a story about the secret societies of southern Italy that listed the mafia as one of those secret bands. But for most of the 1880s, accounts assumed that the mafia was confined to Italy. Even at the decade's end, when a murder in New York City in 1888 convinced the police in that city that the mafia had arrived in the United States, the *Daily Inter Ocean* assured its Chicago readers that "prominent Italians" in the city did not believe the mafia problem had spread to the shores of Lake Michigan. But, while the *Daily Inter Ocean* quoted the Italian consul in Chicago to the effect that even in Sicily the mafia had been wiped out by the forces of Italian unification, the *Chicago Tribune* had grave doubts and grimly warned that the mafia almost certainly had infected Chicago.[25]

In 1885 the mafia may have posed no threat, but Italians increasingly were perceived with deep suspicion. Across the United States news accounts written between 1870 and 1890 associated the people of the Mediterranean with vendettas, murder, and general lawlessness, but by the 1880s they increasingly tied those practices to Italians, and to Sicilians in particular. Statistics seemed to support this notion that Sicilians were uniquely blood-thirsty and lawless. A study prepared for the Italian government in 1874 re-vealed that there had been one murder for every 3,194 inhabitants of Sicily in 1873. Another study demonstrated that a total of 929 people were tried for assassination in Palermo, Sicily, in 1876, but only 74 were found guilty and punished. The subtle distinction drawn by the Italian government statistics between Italians and Sicilians had not yet penetrated the popular press in the United States, so a steady stream of accounts in papers across the United States suggested that recent Italian immigrants were bringing their lawless ways and deadly practices with them.[26]

If everyone from the New York Police department to the editors of the *Denver Daily Rocky Mountain News* worried increasingly that Ital-ian immigrants were a bloodthirsty people who favored resolving their problems without resorting to law, there was considerable debate about why this was so. In Europe a few legal scholars, including the Italian Santi Romano, denied that the tendency to extralegal justice posed a problem. These thinkers rejected the theory that the state should have a monopoly on justice or law and celebrated the legal consciousness of those who took the law into their own hands. On a considerably less el-evated plane, the Chicago express driver Andrew Mattei spoke for many when he suggested the vendetta was an expression of national character. As he saw it, among Italians there was a "supposition that it is unmanly to go to law for revenge on a man who does another an injury. The in-jured man should watch and wait for an opportunity to avenge himself by punishing the wrongdoer and not seek redress in the courts of law." Others were certain that vendettas represented a fundamental failure of Sicilians and their society. The *Daily Inter Ocean* declared that the ven-dettas were a sign of democracy run wild, or worse, explaining that Sicily "is the abode and paradise of the proletariat, where assassins control the government." In a study of Sicily he prepared in 1876 for the Italian government, Leopoldo Franchetti took the opposite tack, asserting that lawlessness in Sicily resulted from the island's entrenched feudalism. The persistence of personal rule undermined the institutions of the state and the "absolute impotence of the social authorities to impose their laws with force" led the people of Sicily to ignore the "distinction between legal and illegal acts." According to Franchetti, the result was that "any criteria that distinguished legal acts of violence from illegal ones disappeared, and what remained were the conditions that made violence the foundation of social relations which were all indistinctly acknowledged in the legal imagination of the people." In an article he published in 1887, the American scholar H. L. Wayland agreed, explaining that the vendetta flourished where civilization had failed or not yet arisen. As he put it, among "a savage people, public sentiment and perhaps public safety demands the exercise of retaliation."[27]

Unfortunately, Wayland's study made another, rather awkward point. As evidence of how "deeply seated" this sort of savage sentiment was, he pointed to the "vendetta of Sicily and Kentucky." By admitting there were vendettas in the United States that were the equivalent of those in Sicily, Wayland stripped away any pretense that the vendetta was a recent, or foreign, import. Of course, this was obvious even before Wayland's study was published. Even as they trumpeted the idea that the Mediterranean had a monopoly on vengeance, news accounts in the 1870s and 1880s made it clear that revenge killings and feuds were the exclusive province of neither revolutionary peasants in Palermo nor dirt farmers living outside Louisville. As one might expect, there were countless stories of vendettas in the South, in Louisiana, Tennessee, South Carolina, Virginia, Texas, Florida, Alabama, North Carolina, and Georgia. There were also reports of vendettas and revenge killings in the North, in New York, Indiana, Iowa, New Jersey, Illinois, Wisconsin, and Pennsylvania. Other stories reported vendettas in the West, in California, the Arizona Territory, and the Indian country in Wyoming. And even cities such as Chicago were not immune, as reports of a family feud that led to killings in the early 1880s made clear.[28]

Indeed, in 1885 the idea that people could or should take the law into their own hands, acting collectively to enforce principles of justice outside the formal institutions of law was hardly a theory confined to a few European scholars. Nor was it a notion that was foreign to the United States. The practice of rough justice was long-standing, with roots in antebellum notions of popular sovereignty. While a few voices were beginning to condemn the lynching of blacks in the post-Reconstruction South or to denounce the excesses of rough justice in other parts of the country, there were others who excused it as a necessary and appropriate response by an aggrieved community. This was the logic used to justify the killing of some Italians suspected of murdering the New Orleans police chief in 1890 and it validated the crowd of outraged Italians who ran the suspected padrone out of town in Little Rock, Arkansas, in 1873. On more than a few occasions, it motivated the often fatal violence that gave Gilded Age Chicago its reputation.[29]

Police Investigations

• Significant developments marked the end of the investigation's first week. On Thursday, May 7, Francesco Caruso identified the body of the dead man in Pittsburg as that of his brother. The same day, the New York City police arrested a man on suspicion that he was involved in Caruso's murder. That man, a fruit peddler named Agostino Gelardi, had traveled from Chicago to New York by train on May 1. He claimed he was in New York to catch a steamship back to Sicily and was traveling with a woman named Vittoria Cammaratta.[1]

Suddenly, Chicago's police had a new theory of the crime: Cammaratta and Gelardi were lovers who killed Caruso so they could finance their elopement. The tale of how the Chicago police uncovered this plot read like a romance. Officers claimed that, before Cammaratta left Chicago, she wrote a letter to her husband in which she detailed her plan to elope with Gelardi. Outraged at being made a cuckold, her husband promptly turned the letter over to the police. It all seemed very clear, but once again, a close look suggests that mysteries remained. The press tended to ignore the detail, but Cammaratta's husband was one of the many Italian men being held in custody in Chicago, jailed on the suspicion he had something to do with the crime. As puzzling, the New York City police claimed that, when they arrested Gelardi and Cammaratta, the two had only $7.50 between them. This hardly accounts for Caruso's missing wealth, and it was not clear where the money could have gone. Gelardi and Cammaratta certainly had not spent it on their trip, for steamship tickets to Italy were roughly twenty or thirty dollars apiece, train tickets

Sketch of defendant
Agostino Gelardi, from the
Chicago Tribune, June 28,
1885, 14.

would have cost another five dollars each. So most of Caruso's famous
bankroll had vanished. Needless to say, Cammaratta and Gelardi also
denied they had anything to do with Caruso's death. In Pittsburg, Detective Bonfield resolved to get to the bottom of the affair. He sent Francesco
Caruso back to Chicago on one train and hopped another to New York
so that he could interview the two new suspects.[2]

When he arrived, he learned the supposed elopement was indeed
the stuff of opera since the heroine, Cammaratta, was apparently
deathly ill. Ignoring the fact that she was, at the very least, a significant
witness to Gelardi's supposed crime, Bonfield let her remain in New
York City so she could catch the steamship back to Sicily. But Gelardi
was another story. He was hale, if stubbornly adamant he had not
killed Caruso, so Bonfield decided to take him back to Chicago. Fortunately, since he had neither a warrant to arrest Gelardi nor a court
order justifying a request for his extradition, Bonfield was able to
persuade Gelardi to return to Chicago voluntarily in order to discuss
Caruso's murder with the police.[3]

As Bonfield prepared to assist Gelardi's return to Chicago, the police
in that city announced they had located a man who claimed to know
about the sale of the trunk. Edward Semple, a trunk dealer with a store at

290 West Madison, told police he had sold the trunk containing Caruso to two or three men around ten o'clock on Thursday morning, April 30. One newspaper reported that Semple recalled the incident because the men were wearing bloodstained clothes and told him they had been killing hogs, another reported he thought the men "looked like Italians." Unfortunately, Semple also admitted he thought "all Italians look[ed] alike" and doubted he would be able to identify the men who bought the trunk. His prediction proved correct; when Semple was taken to the police station and shown the Italians, including Russo, who were in custody, he could not identify a single one.[4]

Tilden Avenue

Undeterred, Chicago's police and press set out to trace the trunk from Semple's store to Tilden Avenue, where Gelardi lived a few doors away from the Caruso brothers. It should have been an easy task. Tilden was a shabby street, only three blocks long, that ran east–west from Centre Avenue to Morgan Street through a small, ethnically mixed neighborhood that was home to the working poor. The building where Gelardi lived, 94 Tilden, was a two-story wood-frame structure that the *Chicago Tribune* characterized as "rickety and weather-beaten." It had trash and an outhouse in the backyard, a fence at the front, and residents living on both floors. Patrick Dolan, a teamster, lived with his family on the first floor in a single room. The second-floor apartment, accessible by means of either an outdoor stairway or a trap door in the Dolans' ceiling, was nothing more than a garret that had been divided in two. One was a bunk room with five beds; the other appeared to be a storage area with no furniture. The windows in the attic were broken and the fireplace was stuffed with rags to keep Chicago's weather at bay.[5]

At first, no one in the neighborhood admitted to seeing anyone, Italian or otherwise, carrying a trunk down Madison to Centre or from Centre to Tilden on April 30. Unfortunately, this was neither particularly suspicious nor terribly surprising. May 1 was moving day in Chicago, the one day every year when leases around the city ran out and as many as half the tenants in Chicago moved house. In days around May 1, Chicagoans carted household goods and purchased the items, including trunks, they needed for their move. This confused efforts to find witnesses, as the *Chicago Tribune* duly noted: "The fact that Thursday [April 30] was the time of the annual moving of householders made the task of finding an expressman a hard one."[6]

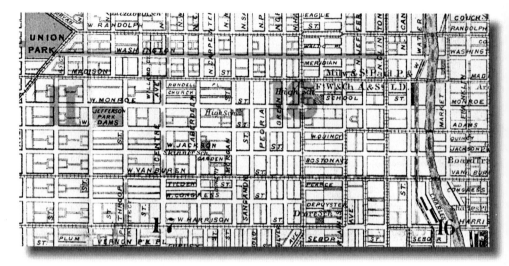

Section of a Chicago street map showing Tilden Avenue and Madison Street, from "Index Map of Chicago: Running South to Seventy First Street" (Chicago: Rufus Blanchard, 1888), from the Map Collection at the Joseph Regenstein Library at the University of Chicago.

But then, finally, the investigation seemed to pay off. Mary Dolan, who lived with her parents on the first floor at 94 Tilden, revealed that she had seen Gelardi carrying a trunk upstairs around 10:20 a.m. on April 30. Her mother, although less cooperative, grudgingly added that, earlier that morning, she saw Filippo Caruso go upstairs to visit the five Italians who lived in there. And Mary's younger brother offered an even more elaborate recollection. He said he had seen Filippo Caruso go into the apartment upstairs around 9:00 a.m. on Thursday, April 30, and that over the course of the next half hour, he saw several of the Italian men who lived in that apartment. One cooked some eggs on his mother's stove, another carried a bucket of water upstairs, a third carried a bucket of water back downstairs and emptied it in the outhouse behind the building. Entering eagerly into the spirit of the case, the younger brother revealed that he snuck up the stairs to spy on the Italians around 9:30 that morning, only to be chased away by a knife-wielding Gelardi. Although young Dolan claimed to know Caruso's name, he denied he knew the names of any of the men who lived upstairs. But he said he called Gelardi "the dude" because he was such a flashy dresser. Unfortunately the inquisitive young man did not see anything else that might have helped the police because he left the house shortly after his encounter with Gelardi on the stairway and did not get back home until sometime after 3:00 p.m.[7]

Suddenly there were almost too many witnesses. A little girl from the neighborhood, twelve-year-old Mamie Corbett who lived next door with her parents at 92 Tilden Avenue, came forward. Mamie said she also knew the Italians who lived next-door, above the Dolans, and that she had seen some of them the day of the murder. Sadly, the accounts of her actual contribution to the investigation suggest considerable confusion about what she thought she saw. In one report she told the police she saw three of the Italians from 94 Tilden Avenue with a trunk on April 30, when she was on her way to school; in another, she said she saw the men with the trunk at 11:30 a.m., considerably after school would have started. Nor was it clear what she saw the men doing; in one account, Mamie said she saw three Italian men carrying the trunk down the stairs at 94 Tilden and then saw one of them put the trunk on his shoulder and carry it down the street. In another account, she claimed she saw three Italian men accompanying an express wagon carrying a trunk. What quickly became clear was that Mamie was no help to the police with the most important issue. When she was taken to the police station and was shown the various Italian men in custody, she could not identify any of them as the men she saw with the trunk. Since at least three of the men in custody at the time lived at 94 Tilden, this seemed to call everything she said into question.[8]

Undaunted, the police continued to express confidence that some of the Italians in custody had to be responsible for the crime. Around this point, the Chicago papers began to echo this optimism, breathlessly reporting that the mystery was about to be solved. There certainly were more than enough suspects in the city's lockups. Russo, who had been arrested on Saturday May 2, remained in custody. By Tuesday, May 5, the police had arrested at least four Italian men who lived on Tilden Avenue: Ignazio Bova, Ignazio Silvestri, Andrea Cammaratta (the husband of Gelardi's purported lover), and Giovanni Azari. Two days later, on May 7, Augustino Gelardi was taken into custody in New York, and the next day, Friday, May 8, Antonio Mercurio, who also lived on Tilden Avenue, was arrested with another Italian man.[9]

Mercurio's arrest was apparently the breakthrough the police had been looking for. Mamie Corbett and a second witness, Dr. D. F. Broughton, both identified him as the Italian they saw carrying a trunk in the area around Madison Street and Tilden Avenue. There were still some nagging problems. Corbett and Broughton could not agree about the number of men they saw with the trunk. Mamie was sure she saw three Italians, including Mercurio; Broughton remembered only seeing two. Still, it really did seem as if the police were closing in. Sometime on

Thursday or Friday, Russo was released from custody, and the *Chicago Daily News* revealed that the police admitted Russo had never really been a suspect; instead he had been held as a "blind" to fool the real killers. The paper added that Russo had hired lawyers who were furious about his detention, and that Captain Bonfield had to beg the lawyers not to go to a judge with a petition for a writ of habeas corpus lest they spoil his elaborate deception.[10]

The next day the *Chicago Herald* updated its readers on the newest theory of the crime: The police now believed that some or all of the Italian men living on Tilden Avenue had killed Caruso at the behest of Gelardi and Vittoria Cammaratta, in order to get Caruso's $350. Gelardi and Cammaratta then used some of that money to pay for their transportation to Italy, while the others split the rest among themselves. Unfortunately, none of the missing money had been located. Nor had any of the Italian men in custody confessed to the crime, notwithstanding the fact that each had been questioned repeatedly, subjected to threats, and shifted from station to station to disorient them and keep them isolated from friends, family, or legal counsel. Gelardi was being no more cooperative; throughout his train ride back from New York with Detective Bonfield he "maintained an almost unbroken silence," presumably because he knew no English and Bonfield knew no Italian. Yet there was at least one reason to believe that Gelardi, at least, was guilty of the murder. When Gelardi and Bonfield arrived at Chicago's Union Station they were met by one of the station's baggage handlers. Upon seeing Gelardi, standing between several police officers on the station platform, the baggage man immediately identified him as the man who had checked trunk Number 4171 on April 30.[11]

More Deception

This obviously proved that stronger measures were called for. Gelardi was taken to Chicago's Central Station where the police began to subject him to what the Chicago papers discreetly referred to as a steady "pumping." That process began in earnest on Saturday, May 9, but even after a couple of days of interrogation that included "a crossfire of rigid examination" and a confrontation with the Dolan children, who identified Gelardi as one of the men they had seen carrying the trunk down the stairs, Gelardi continued to deny knowing anything about Caruso's death.[12]

Then on Monday, May 11, the police came up with the clever trick that let them break the case open. Gelardi was told, falsely, that some of the other men in custody had identified him as Caruso's killer. This prompted Gelardi to make a statement, in which he admitted he had helped Ignazio Silvestri carry a trunk down the stairs and to the corner of Madison and Centre, where they placed it on an express wagon. He also told the police that he had agreed to check the trunk at the railroad station. But even after he admitted this much, Gelardi continued to deny he had helped kill Caruso. He insisted he was out on his peddling route that morning and did not get back to 94 Tilden until sometime after 10:00 a.m. By the time he returned home, he said, the deed had already been done and the trunk purchased. As a result, Gelardi claimed he had no idea who actually killed Filippo Caruso.[13]

After Gelardi gave his statement he was taken away to a cell and Antonio Mercurio brought in for questioning. Mercurio, like Gelardi before him, continued to insist he was not involved with the murder. So the police used the same approach they had with Gelardi, they told Mercurio that Gelardi had confessed. With this, Mercurio broke down. Asked what the *Chicago Times* characterized as "questions of a leading nature," he offered a second version of the crime. According to his account, Bova, Gelardi, Azari, and Silvestri were at the apartment when Caruso appeared there around 9:00 a.m. on April 30. When Caruso came in, Gelardi was sitting on a chair being shaved by Azari. After Azari finished with Gelardi, he asked Caruso if he would also like to be shaved. Accustomed to such offers (Chicago papers helpfully explained that it was "the custom of these people to shave each other"), Caruso sat down and allowed Azari to lather his face. Then Gelardi, who had quietly crept behind the chair, reached forward and slipped a rope around Caruso's neck. While Silvestri and Azari pinned Caruso down on the chair, Gelardi pulled the rope tight, strangling him. According to Mercurio, he had the misfortune to arrive at the apartment at precisely this moment. Shocked by what he saw, he turned and tried to run back down the stairs. But he was stopped by the others, who threatened to kill him unless he agreed to help them conceal their crime. Frightened, Mercurio agreed to stand watch over Caruso's body while Gelardi and Silvestri went off to buy the trunk and rope and Azari disposed of the other evidence of the murder.[14]

Armed now with a statement laying out the details of the crime, the police took Mercurio away to a cell and brought Gelardi back into the room, accompanied this time with Silvestri. There, they confronted the two with Mercurio's account and both quickly agreed that the murder had occurred as Mercurio described. They added that the murder was entirely Azari's idea and that he had been planning it for over a month. Then the police induced Gelardi and Silvestri to reenact the murder in the interview room, and while the two were performing, some other officers quietly brought Azari into the room. Confronted with the pantomime, Azari quickly confessed to having a role in the crime, though according to at least one account he also denied he was present when the murder occurred. Like Mercurio, Azari claimed he only learned about the murder after it happened and only promised to help cover up the crime when he was threatened by the others. According to the police, the three also revealed that Mercurio and Bova were not involved in the murder, though one of the three pointed out that neither Mercurio nor Bova had done anything to prevent or report the killing.[15]

And with this, all five men—Mercurio, Gelardi, Silvestri, Azari, and Bova—were placed under arrest and the Trunk Murder case was declared solved.

The Italian Assassins

As the investigation into the Trunk Murder unfolded over the course of two weeks, news reports frequently confused the various suspects. The impression was that they were fungible, part of the indistinguishable mass of Italians who were bringing their taste for extralegal justice and assassination to Chicago. The reality was different on several levels. By 1885 there had been Italians living in Chicago for several decades, though most of the city's early Italian settlers were from the north of Italy, the area around Genoa. It was not until the mid 1880s, right around the time of the Caruso murder, that large numbers of Sicilians, prompted by a series of economic crises, began migrating to the United States to settle in cities like Chicago. Within Chicago's extant Italian communities, populated mostly by established, skilled craftsmen, these newcomers from the south, often unskilled laborers, were looked upon with hostility and sometimes dismissed as not Italian.[16]

So there was no undifferentiated mass of Italians in Chicago; there were, instead, communities increasingly divided by region and class. Nor, of course, were the five men in custody fungible, though they had several things in common. They were all relatively recent arrivals. The last suspect to be arrested, Antonio Mercurio, had been the first to arrive in Chicago, and he had only been there since June 1884. Like the Caruso brothers, Mercurio came from Termini Imerese, Sicily, a small town just east of Palermo. He landed in New York in June 1884 and went straight to Chicago, where he moved into an apartment on Tilden Avenue. Three of the other men charged with the murder also came from Termini Imerese. The youngest, Ignazio Silvestri, was only twenty-three when he left for America in December 1884 on the steamship *Gottardo*, accompanied by another defendant from Termini Imerese, Ignazio Bova, who was twenty-seven at the time of the trial. The last defendant from Termini Imerese, Agostino Gelardi, who was twenty-four, arrived in Chicago in October 1884. He traveled to the United States on the same ship as the fifth defendant, Giovanni Azari, a thirty-one-year-old shoemaker. Alone of all the defendants, Azari was not from Termini Imerese; instead he came from Trabia, a coastal town in Sicily between Termini Imerese and Palermo. Azari was an anomaly in another sense as well; after he arrived in New York in October 1884 he worked onboard a ship for a while and did not make his way to Chicago until December 1884.[17]

All the men involved in the case left family behind in Sicily, but most had friends and family in Chicago. When Filippo Caruso arrived in Chicago in January 1884, he knew at least one person in the City, Andrea Russo, who with his wife had moved to Chicago in 1882. Fifteen months after he landed, Filippo was joined by his older brother, Francesco, who arrived not long before the murder, in March 1885. Their cousin, twenty-one-year-old Antonio Caruso who also lived in Chicago, had moved there in December 1884, after sailing to the United States on the ship carrying Ignazio Bova and Ignazio Silvestri. Two of Bova's first cousins (both named Salvadore Bova-Conti) had traveled to the United States on the ship with their cousin and Silvestri and had moved with them to Chicago. More to the point, several of the defendants were related to one another. Gelardi, Bova, and Silvestri were all first cousins: Bova's mother was the sister of Silvestri's father and Gelardi's mother. Although Mercurio was not directly related to any of the others, his godfather, Michele Salvadore Bova-Conti, was Bova's uncle. And Mercurio and Silvestri shared a brother-in-law, Pasquale Bova-Conti, who lived in Chicago with the Caruso brothers. Once again, Azari was the outsider. There is no evidence he was related to the other defendants or to the Carusos, though his wife, Salvadora Demma, was from Termini Imerese and in previous generations Demmas had married into the Caruso and Bova-Conti families.[18]

Occupation was an important marker in Sicilian society, and it helped unite the defendants and divide them from their supposed victim. In Chicago, the men all worked as fruit peddlers, but in Sicily the five defendants had occupations that gave them independence and status. Mercurio, Gelardi, and Silvestri had been fishermen in Termini Imerese, while Bova had been a farmer in that village, and Azari had been a shoemaker in Trabia. In contrast, in Sicily, the Carusos had all been unskilled laborers or handymen, dependent workers who were at least a step below the various defendants in class and status. Age, another status marker, separated them into different groups. Filippo Caruso, at roughly twenty-four, was a contemporary of the three cousins—Bova, Gelardi, and Silvestri. Mercurio, at forty-one, was the most senior of the bunch, followed by Azari who, at thirty-one, was Francesco Caruso's contemporary. Most significant, given the public's inability to distinguish among the defendants, there were some obvious physical differences: Mercurio alone among the men in custody was clean shaven, while Silvestri, in contrast to all the others, was blond.[19]

A Skilful Investigation

When Chicago's papers announced the confessions of the suspects, they declared the Trunk Murder mystery solved. Some stories quietly reported two other developments of note: an expressman, Charles Lussinger, had identified Gelardi as one of the men who had hired him to carry a trunk to the station on April 30. But like so many of the other witnesses, Lussinger was unable to identify any of the other defendants. The second bit of news came from Francesco Caruso, who revealed he had found his brother's savings, which he conceded amounted to only $145, far less than he originally claimed, hidden in a trunk in their apartment. Reflecting on the investigation the day after the five men confessed, the *Chicago Tribune* characterized the police work on the case as "one of the most skillful pieces of investigative work in the annals of the Chicago police department."[20]

The *Tribune*'s embrace of the investigation was surely heartening to the members of the often beleaguered department. In the late nineteenth century, police officers around the country were accused of everything, from incompetence to corruption and brutality, and in Chicago those charges had merit more often than not. The officer in charge of the Trunk Murder investigation, Captain John Bonfield, had a career that was especially marked by charges of corruption and abuse. Several weeks' worth of investigation into police department misconduct conducted by the *Chicago Times* in January and February 1889 finally forced his resignation, but complaints about Bonfield had begun much earlier. In 1882 the *Chicago Herald* ran a series of stories condemning Bonfield's "star chamber techniques." Some of these charges sounded remarkably similar to reports from the Trunk Murder investigation, when stories revealed that Bonfield locked witnesses and suspects up for as long as a week, denying them access to friends, family, or lawyers who tried to meet with them while they were in custody.[21]

There were other charges as well. During the streetcar strike in the summer of 1885, labor groups accused Bonfield and his men of assaulting the strikers, bystanders, and passers-by. In the fall of that year, the *Daily News* published a series that accused Bonfield and the men in his station of running a protection racket for gamblers and prostitutes. At roughly the same time two men, one a lawyer and the other a doctor, charged Bonfield with fabricating an affidavit to help a suspect, Joseph E. Sweet, escape prosecution for murder. Sweet apparently decided that a doctor named Waugh had seduced his wife; enraged, he sought revenge and allegedly attacked Waugh, giving him a mortal wound. But Bonfield claimed that, in the course of his investigation into the crime, he determined that Sweet was not to blame. He said that he interviewed Waugh on his deathbed, and in the course of their conversation, Waugh made a statement that cleared Sweet. Bonfield prepared an affidavit to this effect, only to be attacked by Waugh's doctor who protested that Waugh had never regained consciousness before he died, which obviously meant he was incapable of making any sort of statement. Although the doctor accused Bonfield of drafting a false affidavit, the charge was never resolved. It is telling, however, that Bonfield was not called as a witness during Sweet's trial and his affidavit was not admitted into evidence. In the end, Sweet was convicted and sentenced to two years in prison.[22]

In 1886 and 1887, Bonfield's reputation was briefly restored, at least in some circles, as a result of his work in the Haymarket case. Bonfield was involved from the first; he led the police charge on the speakers at Haymarket Square just before the bombing. After the incident he played a significant role in identifying and arresting anarchists. These efforts earned him applause from city leaders and most of the local press. Bonfield had a reputation in the police department as an innovator, and in 1888 he further burnished his reputation when he obtained a patent for his plan for a new police wagon. But in 1889 his fortunes fell. First Judge Tuley castigated him for denying the civil rights of a German anarchist group. The *Chicago Tribune*, a staunch opponent of anarchists and a strong supporter of the police in general and Bonfield in particular, denounced Judge Tuley and argued that the attacks on

Bonfield rested on political motives. But then a series in the *Chicago Times* presented witnesses who charged that Bonfield and his men set up protection rackets and allowed gambling dens and prostitutes to work his district as long as they paid. Stories in the *Times* established that officers in Bonfield's district refused to investigate robbery and burglary complaints, helped fence stolen goods, and punished residents who reported thefts and asked for investigations. Some of the people interviewed by the paper claimed that Bonfield willfully interfered with investigations in order to hinder the careers of officers who were not his allies. His officers and he were accused of harassing political opponents, arresting them and using police powers to close their businesses and evict them. And finally Bonfield was charged with helping to cover up complaints of police misconduct and brutality and helping ensure that witnesses against officers disappeared or left town. Although Bonfield fought the charges, this time the evidence proved overwhelming and he was forced to resign. In 1895 Governor John P. Altgeld denounced Bonfield's methods in his statement pardoning the three remaining Haymarket defendants.[23]

The *Chicago Tribune* notwithstanding, there was plenty of reason to question the integrity of the investigation into the Trunk Murder. Not only were the officers involved—and the techniques they used——suspect, but the confessions that seemingly incriminated the five Italians were dubious. None of the men spoke English and their ability to understand the language was equally limited, which meant the police needed someone to serve as a translator. There was an officer of Italian ancestry, Charles Arado, on the force at the time of the investigation, and like Bonfield, Arado's career was a checkered one. As a youth he had been arrested as part of a gang of pickpockets; in the summer of the Trunk Murder (a year after he joined the department), he was arrested again, this time for assaulting a fellow police officer. Two years later, still on the force, he was charged with battery after another arrest. In 1894 his career came to an ignominious end when he was shot by another policeman during a melee outside a Chicago bar. But Captain Bonfield apparently had little need for Arado's skills during the Trunk Murder investigation, so Arado only worked on the case sporadically and had no role in questioning the suspects when they allegedly confessed.[24]

While it is clear that the only Italian officer in Chicago's police department did not participate in the interrogations leading to the confessions, it is not clear how those interviews were carried out given the language barrier. The *Chicago Tribune* reported that the police relied on "Dago Jo" to translate for them during the interviews. That might have been John Ginochio, a Genoese who was a partner in a liquor store on West Halstead, not far from the police station. Certainly Ginochio later claimed he was the translator during the interrogations, but his claim was contradicted by Officer MacDonald, who recalled that Joseph Ostrella, a local Italian musician, had done the translating for the police. To complicate matters further, the *Daily News* reported that translating during the interrogations was done by Officer Morris, "the Italian-speaking policeman."[25]

There were other reasons to suspect that the translations were unreliable. The *Chicago Daily News* reported that the police struggled with trying to get Gelardi to confess, "for the reason that he spoke a peculiar dialect, very hard to understand." This was an understatement. The defendants spoke Sicilian, and its pronunciation, grammar, and vocabulary were so influenced by Greek, Arabic, French, and Spanish that many linguists consider it a language all its own, not a dialect of Italian. This is not to say that in the late nineteenth century the various types of Italian spoken in northern Italy did not use words that resembled words used in Sicilian. "Train," for example, was *trenu* in Sicilian and *treno* in the standard dialect of the north; "brother-in-law" was *cugnatu* in Sicilian and *cognato* for northern speakers. But there were other words, words that would have been key to the interrogation of the suspects in the Trunk Murder, that differed in marked ways: The verb "to hide" was *ammuciari* in Sicilian and *nascondere* in the dialect of the north of Italy. "To frighten" was *scantari* in Sicilian and *spaventare* in the standard dialect of the north, while "fright" was *scàntu* in Sicilian and *paura* in standard Italian. And some words sounded similar but meant very different things: "godfather" was *cumpári* in Sicilian, a word that was close to *compare* (friend) for northern Italians. Likewise, the word for "godfather" in the north, *padrino*, was similar to *padroni,* the word for "boss" in Sicilian.[26]

In one of the news accounts that reported the confessions, John Ginochio admitted that "the defendants talked in a dialect not pure Italian, and he had some difficulty understanding them." Ginochio quickly added that he "could comprehend what they said," and in response to a question about whether the suspects could understand him, he answered that "they always answered the questions he asked." If this was true, the interpreters for Chicago's police department had better luck than their Italian counterparts. When the Italian government sent him to Sicily to investigate local conditions in 1870, for example, Leopoldo

Franchetti had problems understanding the people he interviewed. And in his report of this visit, Franchetti emphasized that problems of communication increased the difficulties of the Italian national police, the *carabinieri*, in policing the region:

> as foreigners to the island, [the carabinieri work under] a rule of service made for other circumstances . . . ignorant often of the language, of the places and the people, almost always ignorant of the meaning of that rapid and vivacious gesticulation, the rolling of the eyes, and the intonations that form for the Sicilians a definitive second language, which is as clear as a word and which they use to express those things that they do not want to declare openly and that are in general the most important to know[. The carabinieri have no] idea of the customs of the population, of the most complicated relations that link criminals among themselves and with other classes of society, [and so they] live in the middle of this population as isolated as if they were in a desert. They see and hear without understanding.[27]

Franchetti added that under these conditions, the carabinieri made "the same impression as a statue of justice in the middle of a band of crooks." There was another difference between the Chicago police and their Italian counterparts: even the *Chicago Tribune* would have been unlikely to associate John Bonfield or his men with a statue of justice.[28]

Brought before the Law

• At first, the state planned to bring the five suspects before a judge for a preliminary hearing on May 13. But that morning, the prosecution changed its mind and decided to bring the five before the grand jury the next day instead. Several factors apparently prompted the change in plans. There were reports that the criminal defense attorney Daniel Donahoe had been hired to represent Mercurio and Bova. The *Daily News* speculated that this meant Mercurio and Bova had money. In more practical terms, it meant they had someone to plead their case to the press, intercede on their behalf with the state, and raise questions about their treatment at a preliminary hearing.[1]

Donahoe had ample grounds to complain about the treatment of his clients and the delays in taking them before a judge. Under Illinois law, preliminary hearings were supposed to follow shortly after an arrest; they were designed to oblige the state to establish there was probable cause to continue to detain a suspect. If there was a finding of probable cause, the judge could then set bail or determine that the defendant should remain in custody. If, however, the judge determined there was no probable cause to hold a person, the person in custody was supposed to be released from jail. All the defendants in the Trunk Murder case had grounds to challenge their extended detention after their arrests. By May 13, Bova, Silvestri, and Azari had been in jail for eight days, Gelardi had been in custody for almost a week, and Mercurio had been held for nearly five days. Yet none had seen a judge during this period.[2]

The prosecution was on shaky ground legally, which meant that Peter Foote, the justice who would have conducted the hearing on May 13, was a risk. Foote had taught law at Notre Dame Law School before moving to Chicago, and in contrast to most of the other police court justices (typically not lawyers), he was known as being a stickler for the law. When a politician was brought before him in 1878 charged with taking illegal fees as bribes, Foote dismissed the complaint, noting that the law outlawing the conduct complained of had been passed after the defendant committed the actions charged. Foote was also an iconoclast; he ran for probate justice in 1877 on the pro-labor, pro–woman's suffrage, populist Greenbacker ticket. Two years later, when the City of Chicago refused to pay his fees in a series of cases, Foote sued the city. Needless to say, Foote's ways subjected him to the ire of established politicians. When he sought reappointment as a police court justice, he received considerable opposition from Chicago's Democratic Party. He was, however, reappointed.[3]

If Justice Foote was an uncertain foundation upon which to build a case, the Cook County grand jury was not, and it promptly indicted the five suspects. The true bill charged Azari, Gelardi, and Silvestri with Caruso's murder but treated Bova and Mercurio somewhat differently, charging them with murder or as accessories to the murder. Unfortunately, when the five finally appeared in court a week later, someone noticed that the indictment was worthless, because it charged the five with the murder of Francesco rather than Filippo Caruso. This meant the defendants had to be reindicted, and once again the grand jury obliged and promptly issued a second true bill for murder on May 21, 1885. This was otherwise identical to the original indictment. Having been indicted a second time, the defendants were finally brought before a judge to enter their pleas. But there was yet another problem: While the other defendants stood silent, Azari initially entered a plea of guilty. Concluding he had done so because he had no idea what he was being asked and no lawyer to advise him, the judge assigned to the case entered pleas of not guilty on behalf of all the defendants and set the case for trial. Just over a month later, on Thursday, June 23, 1885, the Trunk Murder trial—formally *The People of the State of Illinois v. Ignazio Silvestri et al.*—promptly began. It was less than two months after Caruso's body was discovered and six days before the trial was originally scheduled to begin.[4]

Dramatis Personae

The cast of characters gathered in the courtroom that Thursday morning was almost as fascinating as the crime itself. The judge, Kirk Hawes, was a star in the local Republican Party, and a presence in national politics. He had a reputation in both circles as a reformer. In 1876 he helped guarantee the election of John W. E. Thomas, the first African American to serve in the General Assembly in Illinois; four years later he served as Thomas's mentor while he studied for the bar. Hawes had been a delegate to the 1876 and 1880 Republican Conventions; in 1880 he played a significant role in blocking attempts to nominate General Grant for a third term as president. Hawes had been easily elected and reelected to his position on the superior court, and at various times he toyed with the idea of running for alderman or governor of Illinois.[5]

The lawyers in the case were an equally ambitious crew. The state was represented at the trial by Julius Grinnell, state's attorney of Cook County. A Democratic stalwart, Grinnell became Chicago city attorney in 1870 and served for over a decade. He was chiefly noted during his tenure for recommending that late hour bars be closed; he also took a strong stand against large wooden signs, claiming they posed a particular threat in Chicago's windy weather. In 1884 he was elected state's attorney. There he garnered more substantive acclaim for bringing corrupt officials to trial in the so-called Boodler case and for trying anarchists in the Haymarket trial. In 1887, fresh from successfully convicting the Haymarket defendants, Grinnell was elected to the superior court. But while he was a possible candidate for other elected offices, his political career stalled, and he was in private practice when he died suddenly in 1898.[6]

Histories often condemn Grinnell's work in the Haymarket trial but tend to ignore the rest of his professional life; in contrast, his contemporaries criticized him mostly for other aspects of his career. Chicago's Republican newspapers were the most censorious, suggesting that he was interested more in getting attention than results. But during the trial of the Chicago boodlers the warden of the Cook County Hospital and the former superintendent of Chicago's police force, William McGarigle, denounced Grinnell for having a suspect in that case arrested without a warrant and holding him in custody for an extended period without access to an attorney. Shortly thereafter, Grinnell had McGarigle, who had been considered a reformer during his career in the police department, indicted as a boodler himself. McGarigle was convicted, but then his conviction was reversed and the case against him retried. During the second trial, McGarigle escaped from custody and fled to Canada. More than ten years later, he returned to Chicago, voluntarily pled guilty to some of the outstanding charges against him, paid a thousand-dollar fine, and set up shop as a saloonkeeper. Under the circumstances, it is hard to evaluate the justice of McGarigle's complaints against Grinnell, though the Trunk Murder case certainly suggests the state's attorney was more than willing to turn a blind eye when Chicago's police arrested people without warrants or held them for extended periods without access to a judge or an attorney. Complaints in another case also called Grinnell's decisions into question. In 1886, shortly after his triumph in the Haymarket trial, Grinnell refused to prosecute a Pinkerton detective who had shot an innocent bystander during a strike. Grinnell claimed there was no money for the prosecution; others charged that Grinnell's office turned down donations that were offered to defray the costs of that trial.[7]

The defense attorneys were younger and not so well-established, but they were certainly energetic. Daniel Donahoe, hired initially to defend both Mercurio and Bova, was the only native Illinoisan in the group. Born in Huntley in 1855 to two immigrants from Ireland, he went to college and law school at Notre Dame and then returned to Illinois in 1881 to practice law. By the late 1880s he was one of the leading figures in Chicago's criminal defense bar and was active in Chicago's Democratic Party, though he was part of the reform group that included John P. Altgeld, not the establishment wing to which Grinnell belonged.[8]

Right before the trial began, Nathaniel Sears was hired to represent Ignazio Bova. Like Hawes, and in contrast to Grinnell and Donahoe, Sears was a Republican. Originally from Ohio, he went to college at Amherst, then studied in Germany for a couple of years before he moved to Chicago to practice law in 1878. He was active in the Chicago Bar Association and ran for judge in 1892. He was endorsed by a number of labor unions but he was not elected. The next year, however, he was nominated for judge by the Republican Party and he won handily. Like Hawes, Sears was a clean government Republican; in 1897 he ran, unsuccessfully, as a reform candidate for mayor of Chicago.[9]

Kate Kane, who began to represent Azari on June 1, started law school at the University of Michigan but finished her legal training in law offices in Wisconsin. She practiced law for several years in Milwaukee, where she was a prominent activist. She protested about the way officers in the Milwaukee Police Department harassed the women they arrested and tried to convince the city council to direct the police and sheriff departments to hire women officers. Local papers dismissed her suggestion as so much silliness, but at almost the same time, the Chicago Police Department hired a number of women to serve as matrons for precisely the reasons Kane identified. She also gave public lectures on economic injustice and wrote protests denouncing the Wisconsin legislature for failing to give women the right to vote.[10]

Kane was outspoken in representing her clients as well, and not shy about criticizing judges for making dismissive or insulting remarks about women who appeared in court before them. In 1883, frustrated by what she saw as a pattern of insults from one of the local judges, Kane threw a glass of water in his face. She was promptly arrested, fined, and confined to jail overnight. After she was released from jail the next day on a writ of habeas corpus, some of the male attorneys who dominated the practice of law in Milwaukee petitioned to have her taken back into custody. An editorial in the *Madison Democrat* asserted that the incident demonstrated that women were incapable of practicing law; the *Daily Journal,* a Milwaukee paper, published another editorial arguing that the incident would put back the cause of women's suffrage.[11]

Sketch of Kate Kane, one of the defense attorneys, from the *Chicago Tribune,* June 28, 1885, 14.

Ultimately, the protests paid off and a second judge ordered Kane back to jail; she stayed in custody for almost a month. But while local women chipped in to buy her a purse "as a testimonial of their regard for [her] as a person" and to recognize the unreasonable prejudice she suffered as a result of her efforts to practice law, Kane's colleagues at the bar were far less understanding. She narrowly avoided being disbarred, and the incident effectively ended her legal career in Milwaukee. By January 1884, she had moved to Chicago and become one of the first women to practice law in that city. There, her practice prospered and she continued her iconoclastic activism. In 1893 she announced she was running for judge in the upcoming election even though she was not eligible to vote, and in 1911 she sought, without success, to be appointed chief of Chicago's police department.[12]

The last lawyer to sign on to the case was Maurice Baumann, one of a handful of African American lawyers practicing law in Chicago at the turn of the century. Members of the city's Italian community apparently hired Baumann, who began to represent Gelardi and Silvestri shortly before the trial began. Baumann was from the East Coast and was admitted to the bar in Rhode Island before he moved to Chicago to practice law in the early 1880s. He was more intellectual than activist, when he wrote letters to the editor on political questions he often relied on classical and literary analogies to make his point, but Baumann's work for the African American community in Chicago was not confined to rhetorical flourishes. In 1891 he helped found the John Brown League, which was established "for the dual purpose of becoming a factor in politics and earning from business-men a more liberal recognition of the rights and talents of educated and progressive colored men," and on occasion he spoke out on political and electoral issues as well. But in contrast to the attorneys for the other defendants in the case, Baumann never ran for public office and his practice focused on real estate, divorce, and contract claims rather than criminal law.[13]

Preliminaries

A series of motions announced the beginning of the trial. Kane asked for a continuance to give her more time to discuss her case with her client and prepare his defense. Her motion was denied; the trial had in fact been pushed forward on the docket. Hawes also denied her second motion for a separate trial for Azari. In contrast, he granted motions by Donahoe and Sears to let Mercurio and Bova withdraw their pleas of

Sketch of Maurice Baumann, one of the defense attorneys, from the *Chicago Tribune*, June 28, 1885, 14.

not guilty in order to present motions to quash the indictments against them. But then he denied their motions to quash. Finally, after Bova and Mercurio reentered their pleas of not guilty, jury selection began.[14]

This process was not without its own moment of controversy at the start, as the defense attorneys objected they had not been given a correct list of the people in the jury pool. A new list was produced, and selection then got under way. In most trials in late nineteenth-century Chicago, picking a jury was an elaborate and lengthy affair. This was particularly true in trials involving multiple defendants, because state law provided that each defendant had a right to twenty peremptory challenges, which would allow them to excuse a prospective juror for any reason, or for no reason at all. The state was entitled to twenty additional peremptory challenges for each defendant. In the Haymarket trial in 1886, where nine defendants were on trial, jury selection lasted three weeks. Jury selection in the trial of Dr. Cronin's murderers in 1889 (another case with five defendants) lasted two months. In both cases, the attorneys made extensive use of their peremptory challenges, and the judge allowed them a considerable number of challenges for cause, which raised questions of juror bias, as well. In contrast, in the Trunk Murder trial, it took only three and a half days to seat twelve jurors—half a day less than it took to seat a jury in the murder trial of Teresa Sturla in 1882 and only a day longer than it took to pick a jury in the trial of Zephyr Davis in 1888.[15]

Quick as it was, it was still an elaborate and contested process. Kane and Grinnell battled over the proper way to conduct voir dire; but the greater cause of delay was structural. The law in Illinois provided that "it shall not be a cause of challenge that a juror has read in the newspapers an account of the commission of the crime with which the prisoner is charged, if such juror shall state, on oath, that he believes he can render an impartial verdict, according to the law and the evidence." This lenient standard provided little help; many of the prospective jurors asserted that they had read newspaper reports and formed such fixed opinions about the guilt of the defendants that they would be unable to render an impartial verdict. By the end of the first day, this claim had gotten so many prospective jurors excused that Judge Hawes had to order a special call for additional jurors to make sure he had a large enough jury pool for the case. And this more than exhausted the patience of the press, which deplored the "tiresome" delays and wearisome antics of the lawyers and prospective jurors. Sublimely indifferent to the possibility that their own excessive coverage of the crime had helped bias the potential jurors, the newspapers took the principled position that any prospective juror who claimed he had formed a fixed opinion of the defendants' guilt was engaged in a transparent attempt to avoid serving on the jury. Certainly there were some instances where the facts seemed to support their cynicism. In one such case, a juror who spoke with a thick German accent and appeared to have a very limited grasp of English assured the state's attorney that he had made up his mind about the case by reading the newspapers. Because this answer came in response to a question about whether he had any religious beliefs that might prevent him from voting for the death penalty, the Daily News reported that "the meaning of this juror was so apparent that a smile passed around the court room."[16]

By and large, Hawes shared the newspapers' view that the potential jurors were malingering and, by the second day of selection, was more willing to put his foot down. When William Hartmann insisted he had formed an opinion in the case and he doubted he could hear any evidence that might change his mind, Hawes reprimanded him and gave the entire courtroom a lecture on the duty to serve as jurors. When another prospective juror, Kavanaugh, pointed out that he knew Grinnell, and Baumann argued this meant he should be excused for cause, Hawes made light of the claim and denied the request, forcing Baumann to use a peremptory challenge to keep the juror off the jury. This is not to say that Hawes never ruled a juror was too biased to serve. When another prospective juror declared it was his opinion all the defendants were guilty and deserved to be hanged, Hawes dismissed him for cause but rejected the defense request that he make any cautionary statement to the rest of the venire. In most respects Hawes kept a very loose hand on the reins, notably allowing Donahoe and Sears to use voir dire to "impress upon the minds of the twelve who shall try the case that their clients were not principals in the murderous affair, but merely spectators." Doubtless because Hawes was so eager to seat a jury, by mid-morning on Friday, June 26, 1885, the last of the jurors was accepted and the panel was sworn. This accomplished, Hawes directed the jurors to avoid speaking to anyone about the case and to refrain from reading the newspapers. He then adjourned the trial for lunch.[17]

Presumably the jurors and spectators were glad to get a break before the trial began, but the moment should have given everyone pause. When the newly sworn jurors filed out of the courtroom, it marked the end of three and a half days of proceedings in the case. Yet in this entire period, the five men on trial had not understood a single word of what went on because no interpreter had been appointed to translate the proceedings for them. The *Chicago Times* offered one perspective on the matter: "The three alleged principals . . . all watched the proceedings of the day with intense and what seemed to be a hungry eagerness, following every question and detail of routine in the endeavor to procure a jury with avidity, although not one of these sanguinary brigands understands a word of the language in which their case is being tried." Not everyone was quite so blithe; more than a little defensive about the issue, Grinnell insisted there was so much hostility toward the defendants among the Italians in Chicago that it was difficult to get anyone to translate for them. The *Chicago Tribune* expanded on the point: "Owing to the bad odor in which the Italians of the city think they have been brought through the crime with which the defendants are charged, there is a rather bitter feeling towards the latter, and it is not probable that there will be any Italians allowed on the jury."[18]

Most of this simply was not true. As the *Tribune* had itself reported, Italians in Chicago had visited the defendants at the jail, helped pay their legal fees, and attended the trial. But this paper's guess about the composition of the jury was correct; no one with an Italian surname was chosen to serve. The jury did include two immigrants—Fred Polzin, a grocer from Prussia, and Louis Rosenbaum, a clothier from Germany. A third juror, John Holton, was, like Donahoe, the son of two immigrants from Ireland. Three members of the panel, including Polzin, were grocers. Two others, Rosenbaum and Charles McMahon, worked in stores; the former sold clothing, the latter hardware. Four other jurors were office workers: Charles M. Rogers was an insurance agent, E. M. Cooper and Harry Jackman both worked for freight companies, and C. E. McClanathan was a clerical worker. F. L. McHenry was a salesman, while J. J. McCaughn, a plasterer, was the jury's only laborer.[19]

Circumstantial Evidence

When trial resumed after lunch, the prosecution gave its opening statement. According to the *Pittsburg Dispatch,* state's attorney Julius Grinnell played to popular prejudice, attacking "the copper-colored assailants in harsh terms." The paper added that the defendants, who had no idea what he said, were unfazed, but the jury was rapt.[20]

Aside from the jibes, Grinnell's opening statement offered what was, by this time, a fourth theory of the crime: The frugal Caruso had saved a few hundred dollars; Gelardi, the mastermind of the scheme, knew this and, moved by cupidity, determined to kill Caruso for his savings. Gelardi enlisted two dupes, Silvestri and Azari, to help him lure Caruso up to their apartment in the morning of April 30; they did so using the offer they would give him a shave. No sooner had Caruso been seated and lathered up, than Gelardi, Azari, and Silvestri grabbed and strangled him. After that, they neatly disposed of his body by buying a trunk, stuffing their victim into it, and for reasons known only to themselves, shipping it off to Pittsburg.[21]

Having quietly written the missing Vittoria Cammaratta out of the script, Grinnell went out of his way to distinguish Mercurio and Bova from the other defendants. He ignored the fact that the grand jury indicted Mercurio and Bova both as principals, who helped commit the murder, and as accessories, who aided those who had done the killing. Although he admitted Mercurio and Bova were aware of the plot before the crime was committed and were told of the murder afterward, Grinnell emphasized that Bova was not present during the crime and that Mercurio arrived on the scene only after Caruso had been killed. At most, Grinnell advised the jurors, Mercurio stood guard over the body only "for a few minutes" and "had counseled against the affair." He then closed by reminding the jurors the defendants had all "confessed to the murder and how it was done."[22]

Remarkably, even at this late date the various newspapers had a hard time keeping the defendants straight. A case in point was the *Chicago Times,* which mistakenly reported that Grinnell asserted it was Mercurio and Silvestri who pulled the cord that strangled Caruso. The attorneys for Mercurio and Bova were quick to make sure the jurors suffered no such confusion by seizing on the distinctions Grinnell drew between their clients and the others. Donahoe called the jurors' attention to Grinnell's suggestion that Mercurio had counseled against the crime, while Sears emphasized that the evidence confirmed Grinnell's observation that Bova was not present during the murder.[23]

Kane and Baumann opted not to give opening statements, and the rest of the day was taken up with testimony from a series of witnesses for the state. Presumably the prosecution intended to use these witnesses to set out the logistics of the crime and tie the defendants to the main evidence—the trunk and the rope. As a practical matter, the witnesses did not help the state's case much. L. H. McMurray, a salesman for Vogler and Genatier, Trunk Manufacturers, was the first to take the stand. All he offered the jury was the ambiguous claim that he "believed" the trunk positioned conspicuously in the courtroom was one that had been produced by his company and later sold to Edward Semple. When Semple took the stand, he admitted he could "not swear positively to the identity of the trunk," though he also "believed" that the trunk in the courtroom was the one he sold for $4.00 on April 30 to two swarthy, cheaply dressed men who took it with them. According to Semple, one of the men came into his shop around 10:00 a.m. on April 30 and looked at a number of cheap family-sized trunks. Then he left, only to return about twenty minutes later with a companion. The two looked at trunks for a while, finally settling on a specific one, which they paid for and carried away with them.[24]

While he was able to recall the elaborate choreography of their visit, Semple was not sure his customers were Italian and conceded that he could not identify a single one of the defendants as one of the men who came to his store. He was followed by John Buckley, who worked at a store at 308 W. Madison, just down the street from Semple. Buckley testified that on April 30 a man came into the store about 10:00 a.m. and looked around. After browsing a few minutes, the man tried to explain to Buckley what he wanted, but Buckley could not understand a word he said. Following a period of mutual incomprehension, the man beckoned to a second man who was loitering outside the store, motioning for him to come in. When the second man entered the store, the two talked together for a while in a language Buckley did not recognize.

But at some point during their conversation, Buckley believed he heard one of the men say the word "rope." That seems unlikely; if the men had been speaking Italian they would have likely used the word *fune* and if they were speaking Sicilian they would have said *funi* or *corda*. But Buckley claimed that when he heard someone say "rope" he was inspired and showed the men some clothesline, which they promptly bought. On the crucial issues of identification, Buckley also hesitated. He did testify that the rope he sold the men was "similar" to the rope on the trunk in the courtroom, but even though he "closely scrutinized the defendants" he, too, was unable to identify any of them as one of the men he sold some rope to on April 30.[25]

Having established that sometime between 10:00 and 10:30 in the morning of Thursday, April 30, 1885, two unknown men bought some rope from John Buckley, while Edward Semple sold two equally unknown men a trunk at roughly the same time, the state used its next witnesses to try to tie the defendants to Caruso. The first witness called for that purpose was fifteen-year-old Patrick Dolan, who testified that he recognized all the defendants because they lived above his family at 94 Tilden Avenue. Contradicting Grinnell's claims in his opening statement, Dolan added that he saw all the defendants, except Bova, at 94 Tilden in the morning of April 30. Dolan admitted he did not know any of his neighbors' names but claimed he did know Filippo Caruso, and that he saw Caruso go to the apartment upstairs at 94 Tilden Avenue before 10:00 a.m. on "the day he was killed." Patrick repeated his story that, before he left the house, he snuck up the stairs to peek at the defendants, only to be chased back down by "the dude," whom he identified as Gelardi. His testimony ended on a flat note when he admitted that he left the house shortly thereafter and he did not return home until 3:00 p.m., after all the Italians upstairs had moved out.[26]

Patrick was followed by his sister, Mary, who also testified she recognized all the defendants and knew Caruso, who came by her house in the morning of April 30 to try to sell her mother some oranges. Contradicting the time frame offered by Semple and Buckley, she recalled that she saw one of the defendants—she pointed out Silvestri—carry a new trunk upstairs between 9:00 and 10:00 a.m. that morning, while Gelardi followed behind him. She added that she saw Gelardi and Silvestri carrying the trunk downstairs later that morning—and that not long after 11:00 a.m. the defendants had moved all their possessions out of the building, though she recalled Mercurio stayed behind. Improbably (in light of the fact that everyone agreed the defendants spoke no English), she also claimed that in the morning of April 30 she had a conversation with Gelardi in which he told her he was going back to Italy to visit his mother. She also claimed she had previously had conversations, also in English, with Gelardi, about his wife, and with Azari, about having him repair shoes for her. No amount of cross-examination could shake her from this claim, but one defense attorney did get her to concede an important point. Reminded that it was pouring rain on April 30, she admitted that her family's apartment door was closed that morning. As a result, she did not actually see any of the defendants bring a trunk down the outside stairs, she simply guessed this was what had happened.[27]

Mary Dolan was followed by two other boys from the neighborhood, fourteen-year-old John Murphy and thirteen-year-old James Clancy. Murphy, who lived at 77 Tilden, testified that while he was going to the store in the morning of April 30 he saw Filippo Caruso going into 94 Tilden. He added that he saw the Italians who lived at 94 Tilden move out of their apartment around 11:00 a.m. that same day. Then Clancy took the stand and testified that he lived next door to the Dolans, at 92 Tilden, and recognized all the defendants but Bova. He added that sometime around 11:00 a.m. on April 30 he saw a man carrying a trunk on the corner of Centre and Tilden. But he confessed he was not paying much attention because it was raining outside, so he did not see the man's face and had no idea who it was. His less than compelling evidence was followed by Henry DeBey, a druggist who worked at a store on the corner of Centre and Van Buren. DeBay testified that sometime on April 30 he saw a man carrying a trunk past his store, while another man walked ahead. But he could not remember exactly when this happened, and like Clancy, he admitted that the rain was so strong he did not see the men with the trunk clearly and did not know if either of them was one of the men on trial.[28]

This parade of witnesses unable to establish they saw any of the defendants buying a trunk or a rope, or carrying a trunk out of 94 Tilden toward the train station, was brought to a satisfying halt when a checkman for the baggage room of the Pittsburg, Ft. Wayne & Chicago Railroad line, John Riordan, took the stand. According to the *Chicago Times,* Riordan (who was apparently the baggage handler identified in earlier news reports as O'Brien) assured the jurors he checked about three or four hundred bags a day at the Chicago station. But, he claimed, he distinctly recalled that Gelardi checked trunk number 4171 on April 30. Riordan added, somewhat cryptically, that Gelardi was the man "who three or four days before had come to him and checked a trunk," an apparent reference to the fact that he first identified Gelardi when the Chicago police brought him off the train from New York. As Riordan recalled their transaction on April 30, Gelardi asked him to check a trunk through to Pittsburg and showed him a train ticket to that city. Riordan was also sure there were two other men with Gelardi when he appeared at the baggage room, but sadly this testimony revealed the limits of Riordan's memory. While he was sure he could identify Gelardi as the man who checked the trunk, Riordan could not identify any of the other defendants as his companions. Nor, for all his experience checking trunks, was he willing to swear that the trunk in the courtroom was the one he checked that morning.[29]

The last witness of the day was Peter Dressler, the coroner from Pittsburg. He testified that he was called to the station after the baggage handlers discovered a foul-smelling trunk, and that he opened the trunk and discovered the body. Although he admitted he was no doctor, Dressler was more than willing to express his opinion about the condition of the body inside the trunk. He advised the jurors that it had been dead about thirty-six hours when he examined it; as evidence to support this conclusion he pointed to the discoloration of the head and neck and the fact that Caruso's tongue was "much swollen" and protruded from his mouth. Dressler added that there was blood around Caruso's mouth and nostrils, and a "substance" in the trunk that seemed to have been expelled from Caruso's nose. Dressler suggested that the presence of this unidentified substance indicated that Caruso had eaten breakfast shortly before he died.[30]

Dressler then inspected the trunk in the courtroom and, somewhat hesitantly, declared that it was very like the one Caruso's body was found in. Opening the trunk, he removed some rope and clothing, which he said he was almost certain was the clothing Caruso was wearing when his body was discovered. Finally, he was shown what purported to be a photograph of Filippo Caruso. After looking it over, he told the jurors that the dead man he saw looked a great deal like the man in the picture. And on this note, trial adjourned for the day.[31]

State's Case, Day 2

The *Chicago Herald* reported that, at the start of the second day of testimony, an interpreter began to translate the testimony for the defendants. None of the other papers noticed this. As luck would have it, this meant that the first testimony the defendants could understand consisted of some inconsequential comments by Peter Dressler, who was brought back to the stand briefly to wrap up some minor points. He was followed by Charles Lussinger, an expressman, who told the jury that he was waiting with his wagon at the stand at the corner of Centre and Madison between 10:00 a.m. and noon on Thursday, April 30, when he was approached by a man who asked in "broken English" whether he would take a trunk to Union Station. The first man was accompanied by another, who was actually carrying the trunk on his shoulder. Lussinger testified that the two men spoke to one another in "a language that sounded like Italian," but he freely admitted he was "unable to recall their faces." When asked, he, too, was unable to identify any of the defendants as any of the men who hired him that morning. And, as the *Tribune* noted, he was only "partially" willing to identify the trunk and the rope around it.[32]

Lussinger was followed by William Hamilton, the doctor. He testified that he worked for the Pittsburg, Ft. Wayne & Chicago Railroad in Pittsburg and was called to the baggage area at the Pittsburg station on May 1 to examine a body that had been found in a trunk. Hamilton conceded that his initial examination of the body revealed no marks of violence on the body, no fracture or injury to the bones of the neck, and no lesion on the windpipe. He added that the postmortem he conducted revealed the lungs were engorged with blood, which he thought suggested the victim had "come to his death by strangulation or want of breath, by violence." Based on this evidence, Hamilton explained, he had concluded that Caruso had been strangled and was dead before he was put in the trunk, but he admitted that no one could have lived after being tied up and bundled into the trunk like Caruso since, ultimately, the rope around his neck would have strangled him inside the trunk. In marked contrast to Dressler, Hamilton refused to offer an opinion about how long the man in the trunk had been dead; he insisted during cross-examination that he "couldn't tell." Yet, as the *Chicago Times* noted, he was willing to state that the body had been dead less than two days when he conducted the postmortem, which contradicted his conclusions on May 1, when he guessed that the body had been dead for several days, though not more than three. In one grisly aside, Hamilton told the jury that when the trunk was opened the smell from the body inside was so strong it reminded him of the Chicago River, which notoriously stank of raw sewage and industrial waste.[33]

After Hamilton finished, the prosecutors presented a string of witnesses who added very little worthwhile evidence, though a few tied up some loose ends. An undertaker from Pittsburg testified he had buried the body that had been found in the trunk and then exhumed it so that Francesco Caruso could identify it as that of his brother Filippo. Two saloonkeepers advised the jury that they knew Filippo Caruso and often changed small coins into bills or gold for him. One added that he also knew Azari and Silvestri, but he could not remember seeing either with Caruso. Dr. Broughton testified that he saw two men carrying a trunk out of Semple's store and helpfully added he thought he saw this on a Tuesday, two days before April 30. When Broughton was asked whether he recognized the trunk in the courtroom as the one he saw the men carrying, he cautiously said he thought so. He was not asked if he recognized any of the defendants as the men he saw carrying the trunk, presumably because the only defendant he had been able to identify previously was Mercurio. Another witness testified he often brought fruit from Filippo Caruso, while a second checker from the baggage department at the Chicago station testified that the handwriting on the trunk's ticket was his. He added that the trunk was the first piece of baggage checked on April 30. But the event was not so memorable that he could remember when the trunk was checked, his best guess was that it was sometime between 9:00 that morning, when the baggage room opened, and the train's departure at 3:15 that afternoon. The checker was followed by Lieutenant Shea, from the Chicago Police Department, who testified without hesitation that the trunk in the courtroom was the one sent back to Chicago from Pittsburg.[34]

All these witnesses led up to "the sensation of the day," the testimony of Francesco Caruso. But before he could testify, there was a dispute to be resolved. Francesco Caruso could not speak English, so his testimony had to be translated for the jury (and the attorneys' questions had to be interpreted for him). This posed a problem: Who would interpret this crucial evidence for the judge and jury? Not surprisingly, the newspapers took this more seriously than they had the fact that no interpreter had been provided for the men on trial, but even as they recognized its importance the papers offered a confused and confusing picture of how the problem was resolved. The *Chicago Tribune* reported that, when the prosecution asked to have John Ginochio to interpret, the defense attorneys objected, and Hawes agreed with the defense, directing Joseph Ostrella to interpret instead. In contrast, the *Daily News* explained that the state proposed Joseph Ostrella to act as the interpreter, but Donahoe objected, and Hawes ruled for the state but directed Mrs. Navageto, the woman who had been interpreting for the defendants, to stand next to Ostrella and listen closely to his translations.[35]

The confusion probably resulted from the Chicago papers' ongoing inability to tell the various Italians in the courtroom apart, but it was not the only confusion during this crucial evidence. Press accounts also garbled Francesco Caruso's testimony. When he took the stand, Caruso recounted that he had come to Chicago from Sicily about two months before the murder. The *Chicago Tribune* reported that Francesco Caruso added that his brother Filippo was already in Chicago when he arrived; the *Chicago Herald* explained that Caruso testified that the two brothers came to Chicago together. Here, at least, it is possible to determine that the *Tribune*'s version was consistent with the historical record: passenger lists show that on March 9, 1885, a thirty-year-old man named Francesco Caruso arrived in New York onboard the *Indipendente,* a ship sailing from Naples and Palermo. They also show that another man, Filippo Caruso, had arrived from Italy onboard the *Indipendente* more than a year earlier, in January 1884. Francesco Caruso also told the jury that, when he arrived in Chicago, he moved in with his brother Filippo and Pasquale Bova-Conti, in the apartment they shared at 75 Tilden. But once again, there was some confusion in the reports. According to some accounts, Francesco testified that, when he first came to Chicago, the defendants also lived at 75 Tilden, only to move across the street to 94 Tilden sometime later. Other reports recounted that Caruso testified that the defendants first lived at 94 Tilden and then moved to 75 Tilden after the murder.[36]

A few aspects of Caruso's testimony were basically clear. He testified that he last saw his brother alive in the evening of Wednesday, April 29, when the two had dinner with their roommate, Pasquale Bova-Conti. The next time he saw his brother was when Filippo Caruso's body was exhumed from the cemetery in Pittsburg. Francesco Caruso also told the jury that at the time of his death his brother had about $150 in gold and bills, money that he conceded he later found sewn into one of his brother's pairs of pants. Francesco added that Filippo wore a gold watch, which was missing from his body, and had the key to the storeroom where the brothers stored their fruit. Francesco explained that the defendants, who frequently visited the Caruso brothers, knew of Filippo's money, sometimes borrowed money from him, and often made remarks about his wealth. One told Francesco, "We have no money, your brother has all the money." Another defendant, Francesco believed it was Azari, told Filippo he should protect the money by carrying it in a money belt. More puzzling, the *Chicago Herald* reported, Francesco recalled that a few days before his death, his brother had sent a fifty-dollar money order to their family in Sicily; the *Tribune* reported that he testified his brother intended to send a money order worth fifty dollars back to Italy but was "killed a couple of days before he was going to send it."[37]

The papers' confusion over what should have been straightforward testimony may have resulted from simple mistakes in transcription; errors are only to be expected from reporters who had to write up their stories on the fly to make a deadline. But some of the discrepancies suggest a more serious problem. Many of the conflicts in the various accounts of what Francesco Caruso said rested on disagreements about timing: when each brother came to the United States, when the money order was sent. This suggests the possibility that confusion over his testimony resulted from problems of interpretation. In contrast to the Italian spoken in the north of Italy around Genoa, Sicilian lacked a simple future tense, with the result that Sicilian speakers used the present tense to express the future. Conflicts in the news accounts of what Francesco Caruso said could easily have reflected the interpreter's confusion (or disagreement) over the tenses used by Francesco Caruso.[38]

Confessions and Confusion

There were other problems of translation during the prosecution's case. The state wanted to follow Francesco Caruso's testimony with evidence from several of the police officers involved in the interrogation of the defendants. But the defense attorneys objected to allowing the police to testify about the confessions; Kane wanted to challenge Azari's statement, on the ground that it was coerced. So Hawes sent the jury from the courtroom to allow Kane to put Azari on the stand to try to prove her claim he was mistreated while he was in custody.[39]

The failings of the interpreters working the case were manifest when Azari took the stand for that offer of proof. He tried to explain what happened to him while he was in custody and managed to establish that he was moved around quite a bit from one police station to another, a technique the Chicago Police Department frequently used to isolate suspects from friends, family, and legal counsel. At one station, he recalled, he was put into a room with two Italians who assured him that if he told the police all he knew they would help him. Azari added that, while he was in custody, he was often frightened because everyone said the Italians in custody would all be hanged. But when he tried to elaborate on this point, Azari "used a term which the translator could make nothing of." Ultimately Ostrella rendered the word as "shook up," but it's impossible to say how close that came to what Azari intended to express or whether it referred to a state of mental or physical distress. The translator confused other, key parts of Azari's testimony. Describing the scene of the skit at

Sketch of Giovanni Azari, one of the defendants, from the *Chicago Tribune*, June 28, 1885, 14.

the police station by Gelardi and Silvestri, Azari testified that the police officers "laid hands" on the suspects' shoulders and told them to "tell the truth." The gesture itself is unclear—it could have been comforting or threatening—but there is no way of knowing whether the ambiguity arose from Azari's description or Ostrella's interpretation. Uninterested in the possibility that the interpretation was inadequate—or biased by the fact that Ostrella claimed he translated for the police during the confessions— and manifestly unimpressed by Azari's testimony that he felt frightened and threatened, Hawes denied Kane's motion. He ruled the police could testify about the confessions, and so, when the jury was brought back into the courtroom, Officer MacDonald took the stand.[40]

McDonald testified that in the course of investigating the crime he went to Tilden Avenue and interviewed Azari, Silvestri, and Bova. He recalled that, during this first interrogation, all three admitted they had lived at 94 Tilden until they moved, agreed that they knew Caruso and Gelardi but denied knowing where Caruso was, and claimed to know nothing when he asked them if they knew Caruso was dead. MacDonald added that, when he returned to Tilden for a second time on May 5, he took Azari, Bova, and Silvestri into custody and transported them to the station house so they could be questioned more extensively. He admitted that, even after they were in custody, all three continued to deny they knew anything about Caruso's death, persisting in their denials until after they were told Mercurio had confessed. Doing his own bit to contradict the claims made by Grinnell in his opening statement, MacDonald recalled that the pantomime by Gelardi and Silvestri established that Bova was away from the apartment during the murder but that Mercurio was present and stood watch at the door while Caruso was killed. After MacDonald reassured the jury that the defendants all confessed voluntarily and eagerly, and that no one had to be given a promise of immunity or threatened in order to induce a confession, the state called Detective James Bonfield to the stand. He did not have much to say. He told the court that, at some point in the investigation, he had a conversation in which Bova denied knowing anything about the crime; he also remembered that during the pantomime at the station, Silvestri laughed several times and claimed that because Caruso was a bandit in the old country there was no harm in killing him.[41]

When the last witness of the day took the stand, the problems with the confessions and the translations all came together. The witness was Officer Morris, and his testimony was marked by one oddity after another. First, the papers could not agree on who he was. The *Chicago Herald* identified him as Nicholas Morris, a "Sclavene" who knew Italian. This was plausible; a man named Nicholas Morris was an officer at the Desplaines Avenue police station in 1885, though his ethnicity is unclear. In contrast, the *Chicago Tribune* reported the last witness of the day was Officer John Morris. This seems more likely; an Officer John Morris was promoted to detective in 1885 as a reward for his work for Captain Bonfield, and the Trunk Murder investigation would have been an obvious reason for such an honor. But the *Tribune* also reported that John Morris was Italian, and this was incorrect; according to a history of the Chicago Police Department published in 1887, the John Morris who worked as a police officer in Chicago was born in Oneida, New York, to parents who were immigrants from England.[42]

Once again, it is hard to know what to make of this disagreement. It may have been the result of a harmless mistake over two officers with the same last name, though it is not terribly easy to confuse "Nicholas" with "John." Or the confusion may have arisen for another reason; mysteriously, given the fact that Morris was the prosecution's key witness concerning the defendants' confessions, he had not testified before the grand jury. As a result, his name was not on the grand jury witness list that the prosecution had to turn over the defense. This made it hard for anyone at the trial to identify him or prepare for his testimony, which may have been the point and could also have caused the confusion over his name.

There was another possibility as well. The turn-of-the-century police department was not above substituting one officer for another during a court proceeding; in one case in the 1880s, the department was caught trying to have an officer who had nothing to do with an investigation give testimony in a hearing about the status of that investigation.[43]

The question of Morris's identity soon paled beside other mysteries. Morris claimed he had interpreted the defendants' confessions and that he did so using the Italian he had learned at school. Cross examination made him concede that his Italian was rusty, and he had never been to Sicily, although he insisted this had not caused any problems. With this, trial adjourned for the day. When court resumed on Monday, June 29, Morris was back on the stand. Then, for the first time, he produced a piece of paper he claimed was a statement he took from Gelardi on May 11. Apparently, as Gelardi told his story in Italian, Morris simultaneously translated the statement into English and wrote it down. Then, Morris said, he translated it back into Italian as he read it back to Gelardi, and when Gelardi agreed that the statement Morris read him was correct, Morris had Gelardi make a cross at the bottom of the paper beneath the English translation. In his statement, according to Morris, Gelardi explained why he sent the trunk to Pittsburg. He said Azari told him he was planning to go to Pittsburg and asked Gelardi to check a trunk for him, which Gelardi did without knowing what was inside. Morris then added that, when he advised Azari of Gelardi's confession, Azari agreed to what Gelardi said.[44]

This was a completely new story. No one had ever mentioned a written statement and the defense attorneys erupted in rage, forcing Hawes to call a recess to allow Baumann to consult with Gelardi. But when court resumed, Hawes thwarted Baumann's efforts to try cross examine Morris. He refused to let Baumann challenge Morris's understanding of Italian directly, and when Baumann asked that Morris be directed to translate the English statement back into Italian, Hawes denied the request, warning Baumann that if Morris retranslated the statement it would have to be given to the jury. Since the jury had just heard Morris testify in detail about what he claimed Gelardi said, it is unclear why Hawes thought this mattered. Hawes did give Kane a bit more leeway when she cross examined Morris, permitting her to ask him how he had learned Italian. But the greater latitude Hawes gave Kane did not do her much good. When she asked Morris to tell her, in Italian, what Azari said to Morris to indicate that he agreed with Gelardi's statement, Morris became "confused." Although she made repeated efforts to rephrase the question to make it clear enough for him to understand, Morris continued to claim he had no idea what Kane was asking. At last Kane got Morris to admit that Azari did not endorse Gelardi's statement until some time after it was made, a point that raised questions about whether Gelardi's statement could be admitted as evidence against Azari, but she was unable to do more.[45]

Morris was followed by Joseph Ostrella, the sometime court interpreter and professional musician, who testified at length about a series of statements he claimed the defendants made to him while they were in custody. Much of his evidence, it seems, was designed to show that Bova and Mercurio were not involved in the murder, but his account marked yet another shift in the state's theory of the crime. Elaborating on a point implied by Morris's testimony, Ostrella cast Azari rather than Gelardi as the guiding force behind the killing. He told the jury that Ignazio Bova explained that Azari was the one who decided they should kill Caruso; Bova refused to go along with the plan, and the night before the murder, when the others planned the crime, he lay sick in bed in the next room. Ostrella recalled that, in another conversation, Mercurio told him he went out to sell his fruit around 6:00 a.m. on April 30 only to find, when he returned to the apartment later that morning, that the others had killed Caruso. Ostrella added that Mercurio advised him that, when the others told him they had killed Caruso, he said, "My boys, you should not have done it," and then asked them if they had gotten Caruso's money (they told him no). Ostrella admitted that Mercurio told him he stood guard at the front of the building while the others went to get the trunk. In a third conversation, this time with Silvestri, Ostrella claimed he learned that Silvestri had not wanted to kill Caruso but did so because Azari made him. Yet, when he spoke to Azari, Ostrella added, Azari assured him that Gelardi and Silvestri were cousins who were trying to pin the blame for the murder on him. And, finally, in the conversation he had with Gelardi, Ostrella recalled that Gelardi told him that after he lathered Caruso up he went to another part of the apartment. When he returned to the front room he found Azari and Silvestri strangling Caruso.[46]

When he was asked on cross examination whether he spoke the same dialect of Italian as the defendants, Ostrella admitted that they spoke an "imperfect form of Italian" that he sometimes found hard to understand. But he assured the jury that any Italian who knew the language well would have no difficulty understanding any Italian dialect. With this, Ostrella stepped down from the stand. The state then offered into evidence the rope, the trunk, some clothing, a watch bag, and a key found in Caruso's pocket, all of which Hawes admitted, bringing the prosecution's case to an end.[47]

Chapter

Justice Is Served

• Ignazio Bova was the first witness to take the stand for the defense. He told the jurors that he had lived at 94 Tilden with all the other defendants until they moved out on April 30, adding that the move had been planned for some time. He reported that Gelardi had been preparing for several weeks to return home to Italy and had bought his train ticket to New York, which he showed to Bova, at least three days before he left on May 1, 1885. Seeming to confirm Ostrella's account of one of the conversations he had at the jail, Bova testified that in the evening of April 29, while he was lying sick in bed, he heard the others talk in the next room about murdering Caruso. But Bova added that he could not recall that any of the other defendants indicated they were going to kill him the next day. Indeed, he explained, he had heard the others discuss killing Caruso before and had never warned him because he did not think they were serious.[1]

According to Bova, he went out to sell his fruit on the morning of Thursday, April 30, at about 6:00 a.m., roughly half an hour after Mercurio left the apartment to go on his route. Bova did not return to the apartment until around 1:00 p.m., and when he walked in the door, Azari told him they had killed Caruso. But no one told him anything else about the crime; instead, they gathered their belongings and moved out of the apartment. Five days later, on Monday, May 4, a day when he was once again home in bed, sick with a fever, Bova was interviewed by some Chicago police officers. Although Bova admitted he was confused and disoriented when they questioned him, he was

Sketch of Ignazio Bova, one of the defendants, from the *Chicago Tribune*, June 28, 1885, 14.

sure he could not recall they asked him anything about Filippo Caruso. In contrast to the confusion surrounding Azari's earlier testimony, most of Bova's testimony was clear and straightforward, though there were a few moments of misunderstanding. When he was asked if he had deliberately stayed on his route longer than usual on April 30, Bova responded by loudly proclaiming his innocence. After Bova stepped down, Nicholas Sears put two other witnesses on the stand. The first, Dr. Krout from the Cook County Jail, testified that while Bova was in prison he was treated for malaria. This explained his persistent, and convenient, ill health. The second witness was a little more surprising. Antonio Caruso, Filippo Caruso's second cousin, testified that he had known Bova for many years and that he had a reputation as a peaceful and honest person.[2]

Bova and his witnesses were followed by Antonio Mercurio, who began his testimony late in the afternoon. The *Chicago Tribune* was unimpressed, complaining that Mercurio's testimony demonstrated he was "evidently very stupid" and "did not understand half of the questions put to him." Certainly his evidence that afternoon seemed oddly focused. He swore that for the entire year he had been in Chicago, he lived at 63 Tilden with his godfather. Consistent with Ostrella's new theory of the case and Bova's evidence, Mercurio testified that the murder of Caruso had been Azari's idea from the start. But he weakened the point when he added he never believed the others really meant to kill him. Somewhat inconsistently, he also explained that he told the other defendants he "wanted nothing to do with it."[3]

Lost in Translation

The *Tribune* may have concluded that Mercurio was to blame for the problems in his testimony, but Mercurio's attorney Donahoe was sure the fault lay elsewhere. When trial resumed the next morning, Donahoe mounted yet another attack on the interpreters in the courtroom.[4]

The problem was clearly significant in this case, but it was a dilemma that extended well beyond the circuit court of Cook County. The problem with inadequate interpreters was acute in U.S. cities with large immigrant populations. Court records make it clear that at the turn of the twentieth century, witnesses throughout the country testified in various dialects of German, Chinese, Swedish, Italian, French, Spanish, and other tongues. Interpreters were needed in legal proceedings of all sorts, from tort claims to will contests to murder trials, and in all

Sketch of defendant Antonio Mercurio, from the *Chicago Tribune*, June 28, 1885, 14.

places, from small towns to growing cities such as Chicago. And the problem extended outside the United States, as well. The general rule in Anglo-American law was clear: due process required that a defendant be able to understand the legal proceedings. In an appeal from a murder conviction, the court of criminal appeals in Great Britain made the point precisely, declaring that when due process required a defendant be "physically in attendance" at trial, this meant not just that a defendant be in the courtroom but "also that he must be capable of understanding the nature of the proceedings." Although there were moments when the system did not work, including the case that prompted these remarks, by and large the courts in Great Britain tried to meet this standard. But the court systems in Britain's various colonial holdings had problems offering interpreters for non-English-speaking witnesses in trials and were inconsistent about what they did to protect the interests of defendants who did not speak the language. One study found that courts in nineteenth-century Hong Kong, for example, were "particularly ill equipped" to translate the technical requirements of due process to cases involving Chinese defendants, who often lacked legal counsel and rarely spoke English. In contrast, judges in Australia sometimes dismissed charges in cases involving indigenous defendants when there was no adequate interpreter present.[5]

Practice in the United States was no less varied. A Texas statute provided that there had to be an interpreter present whenever a witness at a hearing did not speak English, but in 1888, a Texas court ruled that this statute did not mean a judge had a duty to appoint an interpreter when faced with a witness who did not speak English. Two years before the Trunk Murder trial the Illinois Supreme Court ruled that defendants had a right to competent interpreters at every stage of a criminal proceeding. This may have been the rule, but the practice in the Illinois criminal courts rarely matched it. At a coroner's inquest in Chicago in the 1890s, a woman was asked to serve as an interpreter of a witness's testimony. She protested that she was not competent to interpret, but the coroner ordered her to do it anyway. Subsequently, a witness at the hearing complained that the same interpreter "did not use the best of English." Compounding the problem, another person called to provide interpretations at this hearing was accused of asking leading questions, so that the witnesses only had to nod in agreement with what he said.[6]

In "The Treatment of Aliens in the Criminal Courts," a study published in 1912, the sociologist Grace Abbott noted that the lack "of proper interpreters often prevents the immigrant from seeking

JUSTICE IS SERVED 61

justice in the Chicago courts." She found that criminal defendants often faced trials without an interpreter translating the testimony of witnesses against them. When there were interpreters in courts, she reported, they were often expected to translate testimony in any language that seemed similar to the language they knew, with the result that a "Bohemian interprets for Poles, Slovaks, Croatians, Serbians, and Russians." At best this led to interpretations that missed nuances; at worst it resulted in serious distortions of testimony. Abbott offered as an example an instance in which a Polish-speaking woman accused a man of rape. At the preliminary hearing, the defense attorneys made much of the fact that the woman appeared to claim that after the rape she went to sleep. Because the judge could not imagine any victim of rape would fall asleep after the incident, he refused to bind the case over for trial. Afterward, it turned out that the interpreter had mistranslated the victim's statement, which was that she went to bed—but not to sleep—after the rape because she had nowhere else to go.[7]

Abbott's depressing assessment was that Illinois courts simply muddled through, most of the time, though she noted that by the time of writing (the first decade of the twentieth century), the judges in Chicago's felony courts generally did a better job of finding interpreters than their counterparts did in the police courts. But Abbott also found that cases involving Italians were the exception to that rule. Even felony courts found it difficult to find a person to interpret for an Italian witness or defendant. As a practical matter, when faced with testimony from an Italian, one clerk explained, the courts just did "the best we can without." If the Trunk Murder trial is any indication, "the best we can" was very poor indeed. But the defense attorneys' endless complaints about the quality of the translating had little effect on the course of the trial. Judge Hawes and State's Attorney Grinnell freely admitted that the interpreters used by the police were inadequate, but Hawes let the same men do the translating during the trial.[8]

While Donahoe's protests did not change Hawes's attitude toward the interpreters, the overnight recess did seem to improve his client's memory. When he returned to the stand, Mercurio told a story that was much more consistent with the claims put forward by the state. He admitted he was at 94 Tilden the night before the murder and heard Silvestri, Gelardi, and Azari talk about killing Caruso for his money. Mercurio also recalled that Bova was there, sick in bed in the next room. When he heard the others talk about killing Caruso, Mercurio said he refused to participate and told the others "to attend to their own business." He repeated his claim that even then he thought the others were joking. Mercurio told the jury that he next went to 94 Tilden sometime after 10:30 a.m. on April 30, when he had finished his peddling for the day. There, he was met at the top of the stairs by Azari, who told him they had killed Caruso. This news, he testified, "astonished" him, and he asked "my brothers, why did you do such a thing?" And with that, Mercurio testified, he turned around, went back down the stairs, and went home. He added that he failed to report the crime because he was afraid.[9]

Even in this more coherent form, Mercurio's testimony contradicted the testimony of several other witnesses. While Mercurio claimed he just walked away when he heard of the murder, Ostrella had testified that Mercurio told him he had stood guard over the body, and Mary Dolan recalled Mercurio stayed behind when the others left. While Mercurio claimed he had never lived at 94 Tilden, both Bova and Mary Dolan testified that Mercurio was living there on April 30. But the newspapers ignored these contradictions. Instead, the *Chicago Times* seized the moment of Bova's and Mercurio's testimony to provide a new gloss on the character of the Italians who were starting to migrate to the United States. When, "less than thirty years ago," the paper began its account of the day's events,

> the last of the reigning Bourbons fled . . . from Naples, he must have left behind him the seeds of some social corruption that have blossomed into recent imports into America. The evidence given yesterday . . . showed by the testimony of several of the defendants that fear of bodily harm, and presumably of death, was what led to their seal of silence. The stiletto has a keen edge and its point is not dulled in the vivid imagination of the children of the Romanesque.[10]

The paper's glib description of easily frightened immigrants ignored the interesting question the testimony of Bova and Mercurio raised: If threats had kept the men from revealing Caruso's murderers, how had the police been able to overcome their fear of the stiletto's edge? McDonald had testified no promises of leniency were made to induce anyone to confess, but as Bova's and Mercurio's evidence unfolded, this claim seemed ever more implausible. At the very least, the testimony by Bova and Mercurio put the other defendants in an awkward position, a position that Hawes seemed determined to make worse. When Mercurio left the stand, Baumann began to put on his case. Initially he tried to challenge the skills of the interpreters, especially their claims that any Italian could easily understand the Sicilian dialect. But when he called Nicolas Tirol to explain the Sicilian dialect and its differences from

Sketch of Ignazio Silvestri, one of
the defendants, from the *Chicago
Tribune*, June 28, 1885, 14.

other forms of Italian, Hawes refused to permit Tirol's testimony. There
was enough evidence in the record, he said, for the jurors to reach their
own conclusions about Italian and its dialects. This forced Baumann,
who previously had said he would not put either of his clients on the
stand, to announce he would call Silvestri as a witness, which, given
Ostrella's claims that Silvestri had blamed the crime on Azari, meant
that Kane had to have her client testify as well.

Azari took the stand first and admitted that he was involved in the
murder. But he denied that he was aware of the plan to kill Caruso
until the day before the murder took place. Returning to the theory
of the case that Grinnell had opened the trial with, Azari laid the
blame for the plan at Gelardi's feet, claiming that Gelardi had come
up with the scheme and forced the others to help him kill Caruso. But
when Azari stepped down, Silvestri took the stand and he claimed,
like Bova and Mercurio, that the murder had always been Azari's
idea. Finally providing the newspapers with some testimony about
a knife-wielding Italian, Silvestri swore he had only participated in
the crime because Azari threatened to kill him with his shoemaker's
knife. Baumann did not ask Gelardi to testify, and so when Silvestri
stepped down the defense rested.[11]

Giving the Case to the Jury

And with this, the case was ready to be returned to the place where the trial had started: the jury. First, court went into recess while Hawes and the attorneys discussed the instructions Hawes would read to the jury. Here more than anywhere else, Hawes left his mark on the trial. He accepted standard instructions provided by the state that defined the elements of the crime and set out the statutory punishments for a finding of guilty, and he gave an instruction offered by Baumann that explained the presumption of innocence. Hawes also agreed to give another instruction offered by the defense, which advised the jury that the law allowed them to convict based "upon the uncorroborated testimony" of an alleged accomplice but which cautioned them that, before they did so, they should subject those statements to careful examination. But while Hawes accepted an instruction that advised the jury that a statement made by one defendant in the absence of the others was only admissible against the person making it (an instruction that was relevant to Kane's efforts to raise doubts about Gelardi's statement to Morris), Hawes refused to give either of the two instructions on circumstantial evidence offered by the defense. As a result no instruction on that principle was read to the jury.[12]

While the merits and significance of Hawes's rulings on these instructions can be debated, the impact of several of his decisions with respect to other instructions is obvious. Two in particular stand out. Hawes refused to give an instruction offered by Baumann that raised the question of whether the defendants confessed in response to threats or promises of leniency. At the same time, Hawes chose to instruct the jurors that they should find Bova and Mercurio not guilty. With each ruling, Hawes took a crucial issue of fact from the jury. Although Hawes limited the amount of evidence the defendants were able to offer concerning the circumstances in which they gave their confessions, some evidence suggested the confessions were made after some of the defendants had been in custody for a week, which the jury could have concluded constituted a form of duress. Other evidence suggested promises of leniency had been made, if not by the police themselves then by their Italian-speaking assistants. At the very least, given the importance of the confessions to proving the prosecution's case, the jurors should have been allowed to consider the circumstances under which the confessions were made, even if they ultimately concluded the confessions were made voluntarily. Hawes's ruling foreclosed that.[13]

The instruction directing the jury to find Bova and Mercurio not guilty was even more significant. Much of the evidence tied Bova and Mercurio to the crime: Bova's and Mercurio's testimony put Mercurio among the plotters the night before Caruso's murder and Bova within range of the discussion, and they both admitted they knew about the crime after it happened but did nothing to report it to the police. Mary Dolan swore that she saw Mercurio at 94 Tilden in the morning of the murder before 10:00 a.m., while Ostrella testified that Mercurio admitted he stood guard over Caruso's body. None of this might have been enough to convict the two of murder; whether it was enough was a matter of law for Hawes to determine. But this evidence seemed to be enough to bring them both within the scope of Illinois's rule that "every one not standing in the relation of husband or wife, parent or child, brother or sister to the offender, who knows the fact that a crime has been committed, and conceals it from the magistrate, or who harbors, conceals, maintains or assists any principal felon or accessory before the fact, knowing him to be such, shall be deemed an accessory after the fact." Hawes's ruling meant that the jury could not even consider the possibility that the two men were accessories; instead both would go free. But his ruling also had implications for Azari, Gelardi, and Silvestri, since it meant that the jury would spend little time independently considering the inconsistencies raised by Bova's and Mercurio's testimonies or reflecting on the problems with Mercurio's confession.[14]

Once Hawes had ruled on the instructions, the jury was brought back into the courtroom for closing arguments. The state began, offering a rehash of its opening statement. The assistant state's attorney who gave the argument laid particular emphasis on the grisly nature of the crime, the desperate character of the defendants, and the need to punish them to the fullest "as an example to evil-doers in the future." Kane and Baumann tailored their closing arguments to dispel the image of their clients as Italian assassins. Both conceded their clients' guilt, but they took very different approaches after that. Kane tried to counter the prejudice that Italians were ignorant, lawless, and tribal by using popular tropes of American masculinity to describe Azari's behavior. She argued that alone among the defendants Azari had willingly confessed his guilt, in the process displaying the sort of honesty and forthrightness that the masculine ideal required. From this she argued that the jury should consider Azari's candor and willingness to accept responsibility for what he had done, but voting to mitigate his punishment.[15]

Where Kane tried to challenge popular prejudices by casting her client as a lone man of integrity among the defendants, Baumann tried a different tack. In his closing argument he accepted the popular characterization of Italians, trying to twist it to his clients' benefit. He argued that his clients had committed the crime because they were ignorant men who did not understand the difference between right and wrong. This was not merely a matter of lack of proper education or moral training (though he suggested it was that as well). As he put it to the jury, Silvestri and Gelardi were criminals because they were "imbeciles or idiots" and "not legally responsible." Baumann's argument that his clients were predisposed to commit crimes resembled the ideas set out by the anthropologist Cesare Lombroso in his 1876 study of criminality, *L'uomo delinquente*. If this was his source, Baumann was ahead of his time. American journals and law reviews began to discuss Lombroso in the 1890s, and there were few references to the subject a few years earlier. It was very erudite, but perhaps not terribly helpful. Because *L'uomo delinquente* was not translated into English until 1911, Italian studies of criminal anthropology were rarely discussed in the United States in 1885 and had not yet seeped into popular culture. This meant it was unlikely that the jurors would make sense of Baumann's claims.[16]

Kane's and Baumann's arguments were efforts to reframe popular ideals and prejudices to the advantage of their clients, but they also contained some pointed attacks on the evidence presented by the state. They harped on the descriptions of Caruso's body and argued that it suggested he had been dead before the morning of April 30. They called into question Riordan's claim that he recognized Gelardi as the man who checked a trunk on April 30. Those were strong arguments, even if Hawes's rulings on the jury instructions made it unlikely the jurors would spend much time worrying about them. So, in rebuttal, State's Attorney Grinnell took on both, though his arguments were laughable. He dismissed the idea that the condition of Caruso's body demonstrated he must have died sometime before 9:00 a.m. on April 30. Instead, he characterized the body's "premature decay" as a fortunate, almost miraculous circumstance that made it possible for the baggage men at the Pittsburg station to uncover the crime. And he sidestepped the second issue by praising Riordan's uncanny ability to remember faces. Then he turned to Baumann's argument that his clients were imbeciles and dismissed it with the claim that the planning and execution involved in the crime suggested considerable intelligence. He closed by bringing the crime home to the jury, urging them to give the defendants the punishment they had given Caruso—death—in order to "remove the imputation that has been laid upon our beautiful and fair city."[17]

With this, the arguments were done. Judge Hawes read the instructions and sent the jury out to deliberate. Two hours later, the jury returned to announce its verdict: It found Gelardi, Silvestri, and Azari guilty of murder and sentenced them to death. And, as instructed, the jurors declared that Bova and Mercurio were not guilty. One paper reported that the jury was out as long as it was because one juror felt that Azari should be found guilty but not sentenced to death. It had taken most of the two hours for the rest of the jury to argue him around.[18]

Appeals and Petitions

Neither the victim's brother nor the attorneys for Azari, Gelardi, and Silvestri thought justice had been done. When the verdict was announced Francesco Caruso flew into a rage and threatened to kill Bova and Mercurio. He was promptly seized and searched; when it was discovered that he was carrying a straight-edge razor, he was taken briefly into custody.[19]

With considerably less drama, Kane and Baumann tried to challenge the verdict. Both made motions for a new trial, which Hawes agreed to hear on August 1. On July 31, Kane filed an affidavit with Hawes that noted that Azari had been unable to pay to hire a stenographer during the trial and could not afford to pay the $400 it would cost to have the court reporter prepare a transcript. She asked Hawes to order James M. Purcell, the court reporter who had been taking notes for the state during the trial, to turn over a copy of the transcript so she could use it to prepare her motion for a new trial and any appeal she might make. In a counteraffidavit, Grinnell opposed her request on the ground that Purcell, an employee of the state's attorney's office, was not an official stenographer and had no obligation to provide a transcript for the defense. Hawes agreed with Grinnell's rather legalistic argument and ruled against Kane.[20]

Baumann and Kane then filed motions to postpone the arguments on the motion for a new trial. Hawes granted their request and postponed the hearing until September 7; later, arguments on the motion for a new trial were postponed again until September 19. When the motions finally came to be heard, Kane and Baumann attacked the verdict on two different lines. Substantively, they argued that from start to finish the trial had been unfair because the defendants suffered prejudice from

the pretrial coverage of the case, the failings of the interpreters (specifically Officer Morris), and the various procedural rulings that interfered
with their right to a fair trial. More philosophically, they argued that
because the defendants were ignorant of the law and the society that
had convicted them, it would be more just—Baumann added more
Christian—to give them a lighter punishment. They proposed the men
be imprisoned rather than executed. Grinnell dismissed the legal arguments and asserted that the nature of the defendants' actions militated
against any leniency. In his brief comments at the end of the hearing
on the arguments, Hawes also focused on the legal arguments, advising
the lawyers that he was "not seriously impressed with the notion that
there has been any grave error in the case." He did, however, agree to
consider the arguments in the motions. And so, after Azari, Gelardi,
and Silvestri were advised of the status of their case by Ginochio, who
was serving as a translator, they were sent back to the jail, and the hearing adjourned until Hawes was prepared to rule.[21]

Much to everyone's surprise, Hawes delayed his ruling on the motions
for a new trial for more than a month, finally setting the day for a ruling
on the motion for October 24. When the defendants and their counsel
appeared in court that morning, the *Chicago Tribune* reported that
Hawes seemed profoundly overcome by the gravity of the moment. He
probably was. Though no one seemed to notice, this was the first case
Hawes was involved in as a judge that resulted in a sentence of death.
This was not surprising, for executions were relatively rare in Illinois in
the late nineteenth century. In the 1880s only ten men in Illinois were
sentenced to death and hanged. The reason for the small number of executions was straightforward: most people in the state who were charged
with murder were never brought to trial; most who were tried were
acquitted or found guilty of a lesser crime; and those few defendants
who were found guilty of murder and sentenced to death frequently had
their cases reversed on appeal or their sentences reduced or commuted,
no matter how heinous the crime. When a jury found August Heitzke
guilty of beating his eleven-year-old stepson, Max Gillman, to death
with a belt, it sentenced him to death but recommended leniency. The
judge promptly reduced his sentence. Murder prosecutions in Chicago
in 1885 offer a snapshot of this process. There were thirty killings in the
city that year, a high number even for Chicago. Only 48 percent of those
cases resulted in convictions—but of the convictions only two resulted
in executions. There is an interesting subtext to these statistics, however.
Kirk Hawes was the trial judge for both the trials that ended with execu-

tions in 1885, and of the ten men who were sentenced to death and hanged in the 1880s, half were tried before Hawes.[22]

But all this was in the future on October 24, 1885. Kane and Baumann made their arguments, and Kane once again asked that Azari be sentenced to life imprisonment, adding that if Hawes did affirm the death penalty for Azari he should delay the execution long enough to allow Azari's family to find the money to come to America to see him before he died. When she finished that appeal, Hawes ruled. He declared that the evidence made it clear that the three defendants did not deserve to live, because it demonstrated the murder of Caruso was premeditated and inspired by the fact that he, by "his industry and frugality since coming to this country," had managed to save money they coveted. After adding—incorrectly—that he had no power to alter the jury's sentence, Hawes ordered that the three be hanged on November 14, 1885.[23]

Kane filed a motion to arrest the judgment and asked, once again, that the court order the state's attorney to turn over the record of the case so that she could file an appeal. This time, Hawes responded ambiguously to her request. He declared that he "did not want to hinder the case" but added "he would prefer that the case be taken before the Supreme Court for affirmation." Seemingly inspired by a moment of cooperation, Grinnell said that he would ask Purcell to read from his notes to any stenographer hired by the defendants and allow the defendants' stenographer to transcribe them and create a record for appeal. But since none of the defendants could afford to pay for a stenographer to take down Purcell's dictation, no one could take him up on the offer and no appeal was filed.[24]

And that was that. The day the Trunk Murder trial ended local papers reported that Detective James Bonfield claimed Gelardi's and Mercurio's wives had been arrested in Sicily for attacking Vittoria Cammaratta. There were a few more stories about the defendants and their reactions to their convictions, in the days immediately after the verdict. But then the Trunk Murder case disappeared from the public eye, quickly pushed out of view by events both national and local. General Grant was dying in New York and the Chicago papers offered lengthy daily reports on his condition. When Grant finally died late in July, memorials and commemorations of his life and work dominated the press. In the little space that remained, the papers reported on other dramatic national events: major strikes broke out around the country; there was a battle with the Cheyenne in Indian country. There was also exciting news in Chicago. The city had its own labor problems; during the Trunk

Murder trial, the West Side streetcar conductors and drivers went on strike. The day before the verdict was announced, the strike turned into a riot when police tried to arrest the striking workers. The day after the verdict, John Bonfield led a force made up of half the Chicago Police Department against the strikers, injuring passersby and strikers alike in a daylong assault. That fall, labor troubles at the Pullman works culminated in a series of walkouts. As worrisome, over the summer and early fall, meetings by Chicago's anarchists grew more frequent and popular. Even nature played havoc with the city; on August 2, a violent rainstorm made the Chicago River flood, prompting concerns about the city's sewer system.[25]

And there were other murders to distract the press and titillate the public. In early August an elderly widow, Ann Fitzgerald, was found bound, partially naked, and dead in her home on Fulton Street. Although there was an investigation, no one was ever charged in her death. A few weeks later, Con O'Leary—described as a ruffian, but far more notable for being the son of the woman whose cow allegedly started the Chicago Fire—killed one woman and wounded his sister in a drunken brawl over money. Within a day of that murder, Agnes Kledziak was killed in a manner so dramatic it quickly rivaled the murder of Caruso. Kledziak was a young woman, eight months pregnant when she was found beaten to death on her kitchen floor by her husband when he came home from work. The case was assigned to Captain Schaak, who was sometimes Bonfield's ally and often his chief rival. Schaak's investigation, which played out in the papers for more than a week, evolved in a fashion that bore a distinct resemblance to the investigation in the Trunk Murder case. At first, the police were at a loss. They took a number of people into custody, holding them to try and find "someone who knows of the murder and will confess." But this did not succeed; there was a lull while the papers stewed and the uncharged suspects sat in jail. Then, suddenly, the police arrested Frank Mulkowski, a recent immigrant from Poland who had remote ties to the Kledziak family and had been imprisoned for murder in Europe. Mulkowski was arrested on August 30, along with another man who was never charged in the case but whose testimony provided significant evidence against Mulkowski at trial. That trial, coincidentally before Kirk Hawes, began on November 5. On November 14, 1885, the day set for the hanging of Azari, Gelardi, and Silvestri, the jury in the Mulkowski case returned a verdict finding him guilty of murder and sentencing him to death.[26]

And so for all those reasons, the Trunk Murder case, which had seemed so spectacular and was subject to so much coverage when the body was first discovered, faded out of the public eye. The lack of coverage meant no one worried about whether the trial had been fair and the sentences were just. There was no call to reconsider the verdict, or pubic pressure to make sure the executions were carried out. There was nothing, even from the local Italians. Shortly after Azari, Gelardi, and Silvestri were convicted, the Italian consul visited the jail to see them. But in contrast to the much stronger reaction mounted by the Italian government in New Orleans in 1891, when a number of Italians were accused of killing the local police chief, the consul did nothing to rally opinion against the trial or its outcome. Nor did he urge leniency in the treatment of the three, even though Italy was in the midst of a debate over the use of capital punishment. Two Italian priests, Sosteneus Moretti and Joachim Tonisai, visited the three prisoners frequently after the convictions; but they were more concerned with helping the men prepare for death than with supporting them in an appeal. Even the other Italians in Chicago who had helped the defendants during the trial turned away; Kane and Baumann complained that Italians in the city were no longer providing Azari, Gelardi, and Silvestri with help in paying their bills.[27]

Three days before the men were to be hanged, Kane filled a fifteen-page application for a pardon with the governor. The petition helped put the Trunk Murder back in the news. Papers reported approvingly that it did not ask the governor, Richard J. Oglesby, to reverse Azari's verdict outright. Instead, Kane merely asked Oglesby to convert Azari's punishment to life in prison. Requests for pardons were not unusual at the turn of the century, and often they prompted serious backlash, with people filing counterpetitions to urge that an execution be carried out. But here, while there was some support for Kane's petition, it was tepid. Three letters written to the governor asked that he reduce the sentences for some or all of the defendants. In one, John Corbett noted that it was supposed in the streets of Chicago that the defendants would be hanged because they had no friends or money, and he lamented that this was true. He urged Oglesby to reduce the defendants' sentences to life because of their extreme ignorance and because no justice was done by taking three lives to punish the loss of one. In another, Christian Kohlsaat, a Chicago lawyer who later was appointed to the federal bench by President McKinley, argued that the verdict would have been lighter if the defendants had been able to speak English. The third letter, from a person whose signature was illegible, noted the probable influence of yet another type of bias. It urged the governor to show mercy on the three convicts because they had been represented by an inadequately trained white male lawyer, a woman, and a black man, clearly not the kind of "defense which the law contemplates."[28]

The statute granting the governor the power to pardon required that the judge who had presided at trial express an opinion on the merits of the request, so Hawes wrote a brief note that was attached to the end of Kane's petition. In it, he asserted that no sufficient reason had been shown to indicate that the sentences entered by the jury should not be carried out. Grinnell sent a typed message to the governor at Kane's request; in it he refused to support the request for a pardon and repeated his claim that the testimony in the case made it clear Azari deserved to die. In the end, it made no difference; Oglesby refused to revisit the jury's verdict. The hasty note he scrawled on the front of the pardon file explained: "Refused to interfere with the sentence. Nov. 13, 1885, R. J. Oglesby." The authority to pardon meant governors had the power to correct errors of law, stand up to popular prejudice, or provide a remedy for defendants otherwise too poor to appeal. But at the turn of the century it was politically prudent to abide by the verdict entered by the jurors.[29]

Execution

Finally, it was November 14. To aid its readers on the morning of the hanging, the *Chicago Times* printed an elaborate diagram of the gallows. The sketch set out where each defendant would stand (Azari in the middle, with Gelardi on his right and Silvestri on his left) in relation to the small chamber at the back of the platform that hid the hangman. Labels on the diagram helped readers understand the mechanism of the gallows, showing that the defendants would stand on the trapdoor at the front of the platform with the nooses around their necks, while an elaborate system of bolts and rods kept the trapdoor up. At a signal, the hangman would cut the cord that kept the rods in place. With the tension created by the cord released, the rods would drop and the bolts that held the trapdoor up would give way. When the trap fell, the three men would drop with it until they reached the length of their nooses. Then as the nooses grew taut that action would snap their necks, killing them quickly.[30]

The diagram suggested a process that would be quick, clean, and mechanical. And considerable effort was made to guarantee that this was what occurred. The cells that surrounded the north courtyard of

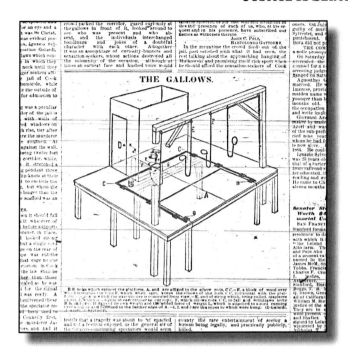

Diagram of the gallows, from the *Chicago Times Supplement*, November 14, 1885, 13.

the jail were emptied for the execution, so that no inmate would disturb, or be disturbed by, the event. The three men were wrapped head to foot with a white sack and hood, so they appeared anonymous and any reaction they had to their deaths would be discreetly veiled. The aseptic aspect of the execution was reinforced by the creation of three juries, required by law, composed of panels of doctors and dignitaries whose duty was to determine that each defendant had actually died. And to make sure nothing marred the dignity of the event, the sheriff's office announced that only two hundred tickets would be given out to carefully chosen men.[31]

That was the plan, but the execution itself was a disorderly mess. The defendants apparently had never been told how they were going to be killed; according to one article, Azari had to ask that very morning. The scene in the courtyard of the jail was no less confused. The *Chicago Times* estimated that as many as two thousand people were crowded into the space below the gallows just before noon on November 14, 1885; the *Chicago Herald* noted with some chagrin that "fully half the crowd were ladies." City aldermen jostled county commissioners, federal workers squeezed in next to ward bummers. It was, as one paper noted mildly, "a heterogeneous crowd," though all those present shared the all-important political connections required to get a ticket to the execution. News reporters, doctors, and members of the juries had prime spots right by the platform, so that they could see the drop and record the time of death. The rest of the crowd pushed and shoved for good positions on the floor, crowded onto the galleys on each of the four tiers that ringed the courtyard, or climbed up on the doors of the empty cells to get a better perch from which to view the scene. Kate Kane, apparently the only one of the defense attorneys to make an effort to attend the execution, watched from a solitary perch on the second-floor tier.[32]

At precisely noon, the sheriff read the three men the execution warrant; it is not clear anyone bothered to translate it for the defendants. The sheriff then led the three out into the courtyard and onto the gallows platform. They were accompanied only by the guards and the priests who had held vigil with them the night before. When the party arrived at the platform of the gallows the priests led the defendants in prayer. For that second, the three defendants appeared as individuals: the *Herald* reported that Gelardi stood to one side and appeared to sneer, Azari prayed with fervor, and just as the prayer ended Silvestri became momentarily faint. But as the three were put in their assigned places and prepared for the hanging, their individuality was officially erased. Their hands were cuffed behind their backs, belts were wrapped around their arms and legs so their limbs would not flap wildly as they died, white shrouds were draped over their bodies, nooses put around their necks, and finally, caps put over their heads and pulled down, like hoods, to cover their faces. Those preliminaries completed, the sheriff, guards, and priests stepped off the platform, and at 12:12 p.m. the sheriff gave the signal to the hangman.[33]

The rope was cut, the trap fell, and once again things went badly awry. Gelardi and Silvestri dropped neatly, fell until they reached the end of their ropes, and their necks quickly snapped. But Azari's noose had somehow become twisted, so that the drop did not snap his neck. Instead, he swung back and forth, jerking convulsively as he slowly strangled in midair. Several papers that had embraced the idea that Azari was the mastermind behind the murder noted there was poetic justice in the fact that he lost his life in a manner similar to the way Caruso had lost his. But no one was amused when the process dragged on. Finally, sometime after 12:25 p.m. it appeared that all three men were dead. Several members of the crowd rushed forward to look at the bodies and to try to touch the hanged men, and in their excitement they nearly trampled the jurors and the doctors trying to record the time of death. It took several more minutes before order was restored. At 12:45 p.m. the bodies were taken down, put into caskets, and turned over to the Italian Funeral Society to be buried at Calvary Catholic Cemetery, just to the north of Chicago.[34]

There was a lighter note. For the benefit of those who had "expressed a desire to see the implements of death used at the execution of the Italian Murderers," Stanhope and Epstean's New Dime Museum & Bijou Theatre announced it was putting the ropes that had been used to hang Azari, Gelardi, and Silvestri on display, along with their pictures. This exhibition was a gesture to the traditions of rough justice, which often featured ritual displays commemorating a community's execution of some malefactor. But some cultural norms do not translate well. The *Chicago Tribune* reported that the first day of the exhibition, the audience was composed chiefly of Italians, who seemed to treat the display as a memorial to the men who died.[35]

STANHOPE & EPSTEAN'S

New Dime Museum & Bijou Theatre,

Randolph-st., between Clark and Dearborn.

The expressed desire to see the

IMPLEMENTS OF DEATH

USED AT THE

Execution of the Italian Murderers

By the thousands of citizens who were unable to gain
admission to the Jail yesterday has induced

SHERIFF HANCHETT

To kindly loan this Museum for exhibition purposes

The Three Identical Ropes

At the ends of which GILARDO, AZZRO, and SYL-
VESTRI,

The Stranglers

OF

Filippo Caruso,

Paid the penalty of their crime, together with other
implements used at the executions.

These silent executors of THE MAJESTY OF THE
LAW will be placed on exhibition

Today (Sunday),

And are in exactly the same condition as when taken
from the necks of the dead murderers, with
the Hangman's Noose, etc.

LIFE-LIKE PICTURES

OF

THE THREE WRETCHES

Are attached to the respective ROPES which ended
their earthly career.

Week Nov. 16th.

IN THE MUSEUM—Pierce, the
Human Electric Battery; Ferrari,
Musical Monarch; Allison Knee,

Advertisement for Stanhope and Epstean Exhibit, from the *Chicago Tribune*, November 15, 1885, 15.

The Triumph of Common Sense

•   A few Chicago papers used the opportunity provided by the execution to draw their readers' attention to some larger lessons about law and justice. In an editorial published the day before the hanging, the *Chicago Herald* considered an argument raised in one of the letters in support of a pardon, the idea that "the limit of the law is never meted out, except to poor men." It was true, the paper conceded, that when murder suspects were wealthy or had connections, they rarely were sentenced to death. But this was not a sign of class bias, because something else lay behind such disparate results. In murders involving wealthy or connected suspects, the killing was not premeditated, as it had been here, rather the killing in those other cases typically was done in anger or self-defense, and jurors rightly resisted imposing the most extreme penalty under those circumstances. While the *Herald* explored the melancholy possibility that Chicago's wealthy and powerful were more inclined to crimes of passion than the city's weak and poor, the *Chicago Times* used the hanging as an opportunity to look closely at popular attitudes toward executions. It did not like what it saw. The paper condemned the enthusiasm with which Chicagoans embraced the hanging of the three Italians, a reaction, the paper warned, that cast considerable doubt upon the city's claim to be a civilized community. In fact, according to the *Times,* the popular response suggested "that missionary effort is quite as much needed in Chicago as among the aboriginal savages who delight in torturing their prisoners, or cannibals who eat their victims." Although the suggestion that enthusiasm for executions made Chicagoans as uncivilized and as in need of missionaries as people in foreign lands brought an ironic period to a case that from the first had been used to condemn the defendants as lawless people from an uncivilized land, contempt for the masses crowding around the base of the gibbet and the walls of the jail was typical of the time. Papers in Chicago, like their counterparts nationally, used executions as an opportunity to criticize the community's lust for blood.[1]

Questions of Fact

As much as they objected to the unruly and unseemly execution, the Chicago papers were happy enough with the trial itself. In this they were not alone. When Judge Hawes sentenced the prisoners on October 24 he began by checking off his own reasons for thinking the trial had gone well. After briskly summarizing the process of picking a jury (which he characterized as "intelligent, fair-minded men"), he advised Azari, Gelardi, and Silvestri that it could not be said the jurors were "prejudiced against you by reason of your nationality, religion, or situation in life," because "two of your companions of the same nationality and apparently the same walk of life as yourselves, and who, so far as was known to the jury, or the court, when the trial commenced, were equally guilty, were, after the evidence was all in, at once acquitted of the crime charged against them." For Hawes the crucial point was that the "jury, after impartially listening to all the testimony and the argument of your counsel, returned a unanimous verdict of murder, and from the statement of the various witnesses and your own confessions on the stand I am unable to see how any other conclusion could have been reached." Justice, to put it more simply, had been done and the rule of law had been observed.[2]

Notwithstanding the general air of satisfaction, no fair observer could have characterized the trial as a triumph of law or process, however. It is possible, of course, that the jurors reached their verdict as dispassionately as Hawes suggested. But there was nothing credible about his claim that the jurors' lack of bias was demonstrated by the fact that they acquitted Bova and Mercurio; he had instructed them to do so. And there were other reasons to wonder about his claims. The jurors may not have been biased against the defendants for their "nationality, religion or station in life," but the state's attorney certainly hoped they would be and consciously played to popular prejudice against "Italian assassins" who threatened Chicago's safety and reputation. Nor was

Sketch of Kirk Hawes, trial judge, from the *Chicago Tribune*, April 17, 1887, 27.

racial prejudice the only concern. Hawes may well have been right that there was no reason to suppose anti-Catholic sentiment harmed the defendants, though it is not clear that there were any Roman Catholics on the jury. But on a jury that included three grocery store owners and two other men who worked in retail sales, it is more than likely that at least a few of the jurors harbored bias against the defendants because they were street peddlers.

Hardest to credit is Hawes's claim that the testimony of the various witnesses offered overwhelming evidence of the defendants' guilt. Most of the testimony from the occurrence witnesses such as Semple, Buckley, or the neighborhood children did nothing to tie the defendants to evidence of a crime. Francesco Caruso's evidence did little to help, since in several respects it was not credible. His claim that his brother managed to save roughly $145 while selling fruit in the eighteen months he had been in Chicago is simply implausible. An exhaustive Department of Labor study of peddlers in Chicago in the 1890s demonstrated that, while fruit peddlers in that city might gross $350 in a year, an income closer to $250 was far more likely. And what peddlers did earn did not leave much room for savings. Bova testified that, after paying his rent and buying his fruit, he had managed to save only $4.00 in the four months he had been in Chicago, a savings rate of only $1.00 a month. Even assuming that Bova's frequent bouts of malaria meant he worked only half the hours of an able-bodied peddler, that suggests a healthy peddler might save $2.00 a month. It may, of course, have been the case that Filippo Caruso was extraordinarily hardworking and frugal, though this is hardly the image offered by his Congress gaiters and silk underwear, but it is hard to imagine he could have saved as much as $4.00 a month. Yet, even if he had done so, this would have given him savings in eighteen months of less than half the sum that Francesco Caruso claimed he found sewn into his brother's spare pair of pants.[3]

There were other, strong reasons to question their guilt, individually or collectively. As Kane and Baumann argued at the end of the trial, the condition of the body in the trunk raised troubling questions about the state's theory that Caruso died sometime between 9:00 and 10:00 a.m. on Thursday, April 30. The testimony by the Pittsburg coroner and Dr. Hamilton established that when the body was removed from the trunk, sometime around 5:00 p.m. on May 1, rigor mortis had entirely passed. Under normal circumstances, rigor lasts roughly from thirty-six to forty-two hours. Normal circumstances means that the body is kept at a temperature of about 70° Fahrenheit; a body kept at a warmer temperature will generally go through rigor faster, one kept at a cooler temperature is likely to remain in rigor longer. In normal circumstances, the loss of rigor by 5:00 p.m. on May 1 would have meant that Caruso died at least thirty-six hours earlier, around 5:00 a.m. on April 30. This was well before witnesses swore they saw him going into the apartment on Tilden Avenue.[4]

But conditions in Chicago and Pittsburg were not "normal" on April 30, 1885; temperatures in both cities were well below 70° Fahrenheit. The average temperature in Chicago that Thursday was just under 47° Fahrenheit at 10:00 a.m. and the actual temperature had dropped to 43° Fahrenheit by 3:00 p.m. In Pittsburg on May 1, 1885, the average temperature was 49.9° F. These ambient temperatures mean that Caruso's body spent the better part of the day before its discovery in temperatures that were between twenty and twenty-five degrees colder than the 70° Fahrenheit considered normal when estimating the passage of rigor mortis. The trunk, the train car, and the various baggage rooms would have provided some protection from the elements; conceivably they might have neutralized much of the cold temperatures. But even if they did that, it is unlikely any of them would have kept his body temperature above 70° Fahrenheit or warm enough to make rigor happen more quickly than usual. The most charitable interpretation, which assumes that Caruso's body somehow was kept at the normal temperature of 70° Fahrenheit after he died, suggests he was probably killed around 5:00 a.m. on April 30, four or five hours before the prosecution claimed he was murdered. Any estimate that factors in the likelihood that the temperatures in Chicago and Pittsburg would have chilled his body below 70° Fahrenheit has to conclude that his body took more than thirty-six hours to go through rigor. A conservative estimate that assumed the cold temperatures in Chicago and Pittsburg just slowed the loss of rigor mortis slightly, so that the process took the longer side of the "normal" period, would mean that it took the body forty-two hours to complete rigor. And this means that Caruso died around 11:00 p.m. on April 29.[5]

Of course, "normal" sets a guideline and cannot explain a particular case. If the only evidence about the body was that rigor had passed when the trunk was opened, this would not have conclusively contradicted the state's theory of Caruso's time of death, though it should have been enough to raise an element of reasonable doubt. But other aspects of the condition of Caruso's body suggest that he died before 10:00 a.m. on April 30. The standard description of his corpse—a darkened, almost black face, a swollen and protruding tongue, effluvia around the mouth and nose, and engorged lungs—could lead to the conclusion that the victim died of strangulation. But the lack of any marks on the neck or injury to the throat should have led the examining doctors to wonder about this conclusion. As one late nineteenth-century handbook on medical jurisprudence warned, there "is nothing sufficient to justify a medical witness in stating that death has proceeded from strangulation, if there should be no appearance of lividity, ecchymosis, or other violence about the neck or face of the deceased." The same handbook noted that a swollen and protruding tongue was typically a sign that the body had begun to putrefy, evidence that the body had been dead for several days. In this case, the testimony about the condition of the body in the trunk—that it was discolored, bloated, and smelled so strong that it stank up the baggage room at the Pittsburg station—strongly suggests that Caruso's body had been decomposing for several days before it was found. Here, climate matters once again, since bodies typically decompose more slowly when they are kept in the cold. So the fact that the body in the trunk had decomposed to a noticeable degree increases the likelihood that Caruso had died well before 10:00 a.m. on April 30.[6]

Other, minor details about the condition of the body raise questions about Caruso's death. Why, if Caruso had been lathered up right before his death, was his corpse described as clean shaven? Surely the defendants did not shave him after he was dead. How was it possible that the doctors who performed the autopsy and the coroner's jury, upon viewing his body and hearing the medical testimony, could find no evidence of harm to Caruso's neck or bruising of his body if he had been grabbed and strangled in the rough and ready manner described by Mercurio? Of course, if Caruso was dead before 9:00 or 10:00 a.m. on April 30 this totally contradicted the evidence of the Dolans and the other neighborhood witnesses who said they saw Caruso in the morning of April 30. How can those contradictions be explained? The simple answer is that witnesses sometimes lie. Given the extensive reports of Bonfield's practices of shaking down merchants and manipulating witness testimony, it is entirely possible that the men under his command induced some or all of the various witnesses in this case to do precisely that. Their discomfort about lying under oath may, in turn, explain why so many of the witnesses gave such tentative and inconclusive testimony.

Confessions?

Of course, it was easy for the jury and the press to ignore these issues or fail to consider the inconsistencies because the defendants admitted that they killed Caruso in the morning of April 30. The evidentiary force of a confession is hard to ignore in any circumstance, and the confession's persuasive impact is particularly great in criminal trials. As one turn-of-the-century handbook of evidence put it, "the introduction of a confession makes the other aspects of a trial in court superfluous." The criminal justice system assumes that no one would confess to a crime that he or she did not commit, especially, as here, when death was a potential penalty for the crime. And while it is possible that these defendants might not have understood the charges or the possible penalty they faced at the time they confessed in the police station, surely they would have understood by the time of trial and would not have been put on the stand by their lawyers in order to confess, falsely, again.[7]

Yet false confessions—and convictions that rest on them—have been a problem for criminal justice throughout U.S. history. As this book was going to press, newspapers in Chicago were full of the story of Jerry Hobbs, who had been convicted of the murder of his daughter and her small friend and imprisoned for more than five years, only to be released based on DNA evidence. Hobbs's conviction rested on the fact that he had confessed to the crime, a confession he claimed he made under duress after being questioned for more than twenty hours by police. More than 150 years before Jerry Hobbs's false confession led to his conviction, three brothers named Trailor from Springfield, Illinois, were put on trial for murdering a man named Fisher. One brother, Henry, testified for the state and swore to the facts of the murder, implicating himself and his brothers completely in the crime and the hiding of the body, which had not been located at the time of trial. But one witness for the defense testified that the victim in fact remained alive and had simply left town. His testimony was compelling enough that it created a reasonable doubt; as a result the defendants were discharged. Because most people believed the brother's testimony, they assumed the three really were guilty and that the legal system had failed. Then, three days after the trial, the alleged victim appeared alive and well. Thirty years after the Trailor trial, an anonymous author writing in the *Albany Law Journal* argued the outcome in the case demonstrated that confessions were utterly worthless. Suspects, he suggested, might be "worried into an admission of guilt, or induced to confess, in the hope of obtaining a pardon." In 1931 the Wickersham Commission appointed by President Hoover published *The Report on Lawlessness in American Law Enforcement,* which agreed. The report concluded that, as often as not, police manipulated suspects' fears in order to coerce confessions.[8]

Recent studies have confirmed that false confessions pose a significant problem, especially in capital cases. One study looked at capital cases decided in the United States between 1900 and 1985 and identified 350 erroneous convictions. Of those erroneous convictions, the study found that 49 percent were the result of coerced or otherwise false confessions.[9] This study and others like it have identified a number of factors that help induce false confessions. Several were in play during the investigation into the Trunk Murder:

* People who are held in custody for a long time or interrogated for an extended period are more likely to confess falsely. In the Trunk Murder case, three defendants who confessed were in custody for over a week; a fourth, Gelardi, was held for nearly five days. Even Mercurio, the last of the defendants to be arrested, was in custody for three days. And all of them were repeatedly interrogated during their incarceration.[10]

* People are more likely to confess to crimes they did not commit if they are falsely told by the police that the investigators have evidence that tie them to the crime.[11] In the Trunk Murder case, the police told the newspapers, they finally induced Gelardi to confess by telling him, falsely, that some of the other men in custody had identified him as the murderer. They tricked Mercurio into confessing by telling him, inaccurately, that

Gelardi had implicated him in the crime. This confession then laid the groundwork for the other confessions, when Silvestri and Gelardi were told that Mercurio had accused them of killing Caruso.

* People who have been weakened by earlier confrontational interrogations are more likely to confess falsely if the police offer them an excuse for their actions or suggest they committed the crime under provocation, peer pressure, or some other external factor.[12] In the Trunk Murder case, Kane argued that Azari was subject to physical coercion. Even accepting Hawes's conclusion that she failed to prove this claim, the evidence suggests that at some point during the investigation he was put in a room with other Italians (presumably some or all of the "interpreters") who encouraged him to confess. It is also, perhaps, significant that several of the defendants claimed they only agreed to help with the murder when they were threatened, statements that might demonstrate that the police's leading questions helped plant this justification in their minds.

* People who are particularly vulnerable to authority such as children, teenagers, or members of minority groups, or people who are unsophisticated legally, are more likely to confess falsely. Everyone agreed that the defendants in the Trunk Murder case were ignorant of the law and the language in which they were being questioned. The men had been kept isolated while they were in custody and not permitted to see family or friends, who might have brought them legal assistance. There was also evidence they were confused about the possible punishment they might receive; one paper reported that the defendants had been told that, if they confessed, they would not be executed.[13]

This suggests that the defendants were the sort of people who could be induced to confess falsely at the police station, but what of the fact that Azari and Silvestri reaffirmed their confessions at trial? What of the fact that Bova and Mercurio testified at trial, under oath, that they knew the others committed the murder? As testimony made under oath on the advice of counsel, these statements may seem both credible and damning, but the Trailor case reminds us that the fact a confession is made in court is not proof it is accurate. In that case, as was true with the confessions of Bova and Mercurio, the statements blamed others and helped convince the state to recommend lenient treatment for the confessors. As the self-serving statements of men who were themselves charged with Caruso's murder, these were the sort of statements that Anglo-American common law has long considered suspect and often barred.[14]

In contrast, the statements by Azari and Silvestri were not self-serving; they were the sort of admissions against interest that the criminal justice system has usually considered particularly trustworthy. But they were also statements made on the advice of counsel who could not communicate easily with their clients and by defendants who, because of the problems with interpreters, may have understood little of the testimony or evidence against them. And they were statements made by men who had already been convicted in the press and had just been accused by their codefendants. Attorneys have been known to conclude, wrongly, that their client committed a crime and pressured their client to confess in the hope that doing so would encourage the judge or jury to be more lenient. Other attorneys have calculated that the likelihood their client would be treated leniently would increase if the client confessed to a crime, regardless of whether he or she had committed it. Something of the sort was Kane's strategy at trial, as her closing argument emphasizing Azari's willingness to accept responsibility for the crime made clear. And it was not an uncommon approach. Robert Ferrari, a criminal defense attorney who represented immigrant defendants in New York in the early part of the twentieth century, stated, there were "many occasions upon which it would be cruel and criminal on the part of the lawyer not to advise his client to plead guilty. And this is irrespective of whether the client is guilty or not."[15]

Another legal scholar writing about the reliability of confessions in 1875 worried about what this sort of logic meant for the criminal justice system as a whole. He argued that in-court confessions were no more trustworthy than those made out of court, to the extent that both types of confessions needed to be corroborated by other evidence. In either case, he added, there should be "close scrutiny of the circumstances of the confession, the mental and physical conditions of the accused, and the influences which have been brought to bear in producing the confession." The opposite happened in the Trunk Murder case, where the circumstantial evidence was too weak to convict and had to be corroborated by the statements of the defendants.[16]

Due Process of Law

When he sentenced Azari, Gelardi, and Silvestri, Hawes advised them, "You have had a fair and impartial trial. No evidence in your behalf was excluded that in any degree tended to establish your innocence, while the public prosecutor, in seeking your conviction, was held to the strict compliance with all the rules of evidence governing trials of this character."[17] But really, there were legal problems from the start.

Certainly, the arrests and detentions of the various Italians made between May 1 and May 10, 1885, were of dubious legality. Under Illinois law, a police officer could only arrest a person within his jurisdiction, and this meant there were problems when Detective Bonfield took Gelardi into custody in New York, a city that was clearly outside the scope of his authority. The proper course would have been for Bonfield to seek to extradite Gelardi under Article IV, section 2, of the U.S. Constitution. The Supreme Court had interpreted this article to mean that the "Executive authority [of the state seeking extradition] was not authorized by this article to make the demand unless the party was charged in the regular course of judicial proceedings." In plain language, Illinois could not legally demand that New York turn Gelardi over to Bonfield without a warrant or other documentation that charges had been filed against him. Bonfield, of course, had neither. He got around this requirement by claiming that Gelardi had agreed voluntarily to return to Chicago. Given Gelardi's problems with the English language and his lack of understanding of American law, it is unlikely this claim would have stood up on appeal.[18]

It also is likely that the Illinois Supreme Court would have questioned the way Hawes conducted the preliminary hearing. Since the first Illinois Constitution, written in 1818, the rule had been that "in all criminal proceedings the accused shall have a right to be heard by himself and counsel." By statute, "every person charged with a crime" had a right to have counsel appointed for him if he stated "under oath that he is unable to procure counsel." The Illinois Supreme Court interpreted this statute to mean that defendants were entitled to counsel at arraignment and also concluded that the statute imposed on trial judges a "duty . . . to assign counsel to defend persons charged with a crime, who were unable to employ counsel." The Illinois Supreme Court also had declared that, where defendants in a criminal case did not understand English and were unfamiliar with American legal processes, the judge conducting the hearing should appoint an attorney and find a suitable interpreter during the preliminary hearing. Even though only two of the defendants, Mercurio and Bova, had counsel at the preliminary hearing, Hawes did not appoint counsel to represent the others.[19]

Hawes's rulings through the course of the trial were just as suspect. Kane opened the trial with a motion to try the defendants separately. The basic rule in Illinois was that jointly indicted defendants should be tried together, and any decision to give the defendants separate trials was within the discretion of the trial judge. But this general rule had been circumscribed in 1879 in *White v. Illinois*, where the Illinois Supreme Court held that, if the evidence of one defendant was very damaging to another, a motion for separate trials should be granted. By the end of the nineteenth century, Illinois courts had begun to read *White* narrowly, sustaining judges who denied motions to give defendants separate trials. But in 1885, just six years after *White* had been decided and with no decisions limiting its scope, the case meant that Kane had reasonable grounds to request a separate trial for Azari and strong grounds for an appeal based on Hawes's decision to deny the request.[20]

Kane also filed a motion for a continuance, arguing that she needed more time to prepare. Her motion pointed out that she had not begun to represent Azari until June 1, and for two weeks thereafter she was unable to prepare her case because she could not communicate with Azari directly and could not find anyone who was able to interpret his Sicilian. Once again, the general rule was that the decision to grant such a motion was a matter within the trial judge's discretion. But the Illinois Supreme Court had shown itself more than willing to reverse cases where trial judges denied this sort of motion. In *Illinois v. Dacey*, a case decided the year before the Trunk Murder trial, the Illinois Supreme Court held that "[c]ontinuances ought always to be granted when, from the showing [in the motion], justice requires it be done, and to enable a defendant to procure all legal and competent evidence necessary for the fair presentation of his case, if he has used due diligence to obtain the same." In *Dacey*, the court denied the request for a continuance, noting that the evidence sought by the defendant "would be cumulative, merely" to testimony of witnesses who were available to testify. The court emphasized that Dacey had over ten days to reach the witnesses, who were in the neighboring state of Iowa, and it would take them only two days to get to court once they were contacted.[21]

Ultimately, the result in *Dacey* turned on the Illinois Supreme Court's conclusion that the limited value of the testimony that would be offered by the missing witnesses' testimony—coupled with consideration of the length of time the defendant had had available to get hold of the missing witness—meant that a continuance would not have helped the defendant's case. This was consistent with the rule the Illinois Supreme Court had set down in an earlier case, *Conley v. Illinois*. In *Conley*, the supreme court reversed the trial judge's decision to deny the motion for a continuance. Explaining this ruling, the supreme court emphasized that the five days between the time the defendant was arrested for gambling and the time he was brought to trial did not give his attorney enough time to prepare a defense. And so the court concluded that the request for a continuance should have been granted. In *Conley* the actual charges were not terribly serious; in cases where the crimes at issue were more serious and the potential punishments greater, the Illinois Supreme Court held that even periods longer than five days were not enough to allow for adequate preparation.[22]

These cases suggest that the decision to grant a continuance should turn on two points: whether the defense had been reasonably diligent in preparing for trial and whether the evidence that would be obtained by a delay was important to the defense case. The Illinois Supreme Court made it clear that extraordinary circumstances could modify these requirements. In *Wray v. Illinois,* where defense counsel resigned on the eve of the trial, the court held that a continuance should be granted in a retrial without regard to the materiality of the evidence offered by the witnesses that defendant had been trying to locate. In the Trunk Murder trial, Kane sought a continuance based on the delays caused by her inability to communicate with her client and by the fact that she was trying to establish contact with Azari's family in Italy in order to trace out his claim that the crime had Italian roots. Either problem would seem to fit the case within the scope of the cases from *Conley* to *Dacey* and suggested that on appeal the Illinois Supreme Court would have ruled it was an error for Hawes to refuse to grant her request for an extension of time.[23]

The defense attorneys were on the firmest ground when they complained about problems with the interpreters at the trial. The Illinois Supreme Court had noted the importance of accurate translations in criminal trials as early as 1859, when it ruled that any defendant who objected to a translation offered against him should be entitled to offer an alternative translation. This case might be read as merely requiring that jurors have access to accurate translations, but even this minimum standard was not consistently met in the Trunk Murder trial. More to the point, subsequent cases made it clear that the standard was higher than that. In 1883 the Illinois Supreme Court established that people charged with crimes had a right to translators to help them understand all the legal proceedings involving them. In that case, *Gardner v. Illinois,* the supreme court held that a trial judge should not have accepted a guilty plea from a defendant who was a recent immigrant from Germany and knew virtually no English. The court explained that when the crime charged was serious and the defendant foreign-born, with little knowledge of either the English language or the American criminal processes, an interpreter was necessary at every stage of a criminal proceeding. The defendants in the Trunk Murder case were as much in need of competent translations as the defendant in *Gardner,* and yet they did not have any interpreters to assist them when they first appeared before Hawes or for the first three or four days of trial. And once the interpreters did appear, there seemed adequate reason to doubt their competence. *Gardner* suggests that Hawes should have done more, and that his failure to do so was reversible error.[24]

The problem of translation predated the formal legal proceedings, of course, most obviously with respect to the purported confessions to the police officers. While there were no Illinois cases directly on point, at the very least the Illinois Supreme Court's decision in *Schneir v. Illinois,* where the court held that defendants had a right to challenge incompetent translations during trial, suggests that Baumann and Kane and the other defense attorneys should have been able to challenge the competence of the people who claimed they translated the confessions and should have been able to present evidence explaining why those interpretations were flawed. If nothing else, it was a matter for Hawes to take more seriously, particularly in light of the evidence that the confessions were made by men who had been in custody for several days without seeing an attorney or a judge.[25]

Finally, Hawes's decision to use the jury instructions to take certain issues from the jury was grounds for an appeal. Since 1879, it had been reversible error for a trial judge to take contested issues of fact from the jury in a criminal trial. Hawes's rulings in this respect were particularly egregious because he had been reversed on precisely this issue in several civil cases between 1883 and 1885. In the last of those cases, which came down just four months before the Trunk Murder trial, he was reprimanded for giving an instruction that assumed all the defendants participated in a fraud because this was a question for the jury to decide. Given Hawes's record of abuses in this particular area, it seems likely a court of appeal would have reversed on this ground as well.[26]

This meant there were any number of grounds for an appeal and good reason to hope that, if the case were appealed, the verdict would be reversed. But this did not happen. Once again, Hawes's rulings influenced the outcome. When he refused to order the state's attorney to supply Kane with the stenographer's notes from the trial, he determined the fate of the appeal. But he did not clearly violate any law when he did so. An Illinois statute provided that "If any court shall, before or after the commencement of any suit, be satisfied that the plaintiff is a poor person and unable to prosecute his suit and pay the costs and expenses thereof, the court may, in its discretion, permit him to commence and prosecute his suit as a poor person; and thereupon such person shall have all the necessary writs, process and proceedings, as in other cases, without fees or charge." But while that rule seemed, with its talk of "any court" to include criminal cases, no court had applied it in the criminal context. Nor had Illinois courts recognized that criminal defendants had a right of appeal. So while Hawes apparently could have allowed Azari to take an appeal *in forma pauperis,* he was under no obligation to do so (and it is not clear that Kane ever framed her request in those terms). Of course, even if he had allowed Azari to appeal *in forma pauperis,* this would not have guaranteed an appeal, since there was no obvious way to avoid the requirement that a transcript be provided as part of the record on appeal and no clear ground to order Grinnell to make Purcell's notes available to create a transcript. Not quite seventy-five years after the Trunk Murder trial, in 1956, the U.S. Supreme Court held that states had an obligation to provide trial transcripts free to criminal defendants who could not afford to pay. In this case, which involved two defendants convicted of robbery by a trial court in Chicago, Justice Black declared that there was "no meaningful distinction between a rule which would deny the poor the right to defend themselves in a trial court and one which effectively denies the poor an adequate appellate review accorded to all who have money enough to pay the costs in advance." But this was not the rule in the late nineteenth century. In the absence of a transcript, there could be no appeal and no way to raise or redress the problems caused by Hawes's rulings at trial.[27]

Commonsense Justice

So this was a case in which the legal rules designed to protect immigrants—or otherwise to guarantee criminal defendants a fair trial—were ignored. And this happened deliberately. Judge Hawes believed that too much law cluttered trials and too often interfered with the ultimate goal of a criminal case, which he believed was to let the jurors use their common sense to evaluate the case and determine what justice required. As he explained, in another context:

> What the law asked the jury to do was simply to consider the evidence brought before them in a common-sense way and not take for granted either the guilt or innocence of the accused, but to arrive at one or the other conclusions by an impartial weighing of the opposing evidence

brought before them. Jurors were not advocates of either the State or the accused, but of justice. They were not to be guided by the technicalities of the law; nor to mistake justice as a piece of intricate machinery, devised for the escape of criminals, but to follow their own good judgment and be guided by those instincts of right which guided them in the every-day affairs of life. Their province was to discover guilt, not to furnish a loop-hole for escape. They were not meant as the almoners of mercy, but as the administration of justice.[28]

Hawes often was praised for his willingness to ignore "legalistic requests." As one biographer put it, Hawes would "without hesitation brush aside the mere technicalities of the law, for which he had much less respect than for substantive merits." Nor was the approach peculiar to Hawes or unique to Chicago. The anonymous author of an essay on "The Psychology of Murder," published in 1876, noted that jurors in America and Europe were inclined to substitute their judgment for the strict rule of law, in order to excuse murders that they viewed as moral. Lawyers appealed to commonsense justice in their arguments in court, politicians asserted its value, and other judges embraced it, implicitly if not explicitly.[29]

Commonsense justice was a neat way to bring the community into the criminal justice system, to make the formal law popular. But some were less than enthralled. Writing about Judge Hawes's understanding of commonsense justice, an author in the *American Law Review* suggested he had "forgotten the obligations of his oath, and imagines himself in some way to be an exponent of that portion of the sovereignty of the people which is above the law." Referring to Hawes's statement quoted above, he suggested it was "scarcely credible that any judge should have used an expression as that the office of the jurors is to discover guilt." Jurors, he explained, "are not detectives or prosecuting officers. Their office is to discover the truth." The problem, this author concluded, was not just with Hawes. "There is a good deal of nonsense upon this subject, and every change which is rung on the subject of jury trial shows that it is the greatest farce of modern times." For all its political value, the trial by jury, the author concluded, was "simply a trial by popular prejudice."[30]

In an article written in 1910, Roscoe Pound argued that the embrace of commonsense justice did more than overvalue the jurors' sense of right and wrong. Although he admitted many rules and laws were often inconsistent with community sentiment, Pound denied that the proper response was for the courts systematically to ignore the rule of law or to defer to jurors' common sense. He argued that this sort of approach only encouraged the rest of the legal system to ignore the limits imposed by law as well. The third degree and other forms of police abuse were a result. While Pound worried that the problem was endemic, he argued it was particularly acute—and damaging—in criminal trials. Other turn-of-the-century commentators agreed, and some expressed the concern that the informal ad hoc approach to criminal justice described by Pound posed particular problems when applied to immigrants and other outsiders, because it denied them the legal protections they often needed in order to receive a fair trial.[31]

This was what happened here. The criminal justice system treated Azari and the other Trunk Murder suspects badly because Hawes chose to ignore the law. As a practical matter, this meant he denied the defendants the protections that they, like any criminal defendant, were entitled to, and he denied them the special protections the Illinois Supreme Court had declared non-English-speaking defendants deserved in order to ensure their trials were fair. And this was all it took—because Hawes's approach was popular, because there was no public outcry about the injustice of the result, and because none of the defendants could afford to appeal the verdict against them.

Conclusion

• Writing about the Trunk Murder trial during what must have been a slow news day, the editorial writers for the *Chicago Times* waxed poetic: "The trial," they noted, "is one which presents some cosmopolitan features. The defendants are Italians, one of the attorneys is African, another is a woman, the presiding judge is an American, and there are several nationalities on the jury. It is rather a queer outcome of the progress of events, the meeting under the circumstances of the various representatives of the two continents."[1]

It could have been that way. Certainly, Judge Hawes's courtroom was a ground in which people from across the country and around the world came together those weeks in the summer of 1885. The lawyers were from several states, the jurors included several immigrants, and the defendants, many of the witnesses, and a good part of the spectators in the courtroom had come across the Atlantic. They came with a mix of attitudes, some were reformers, some simply ambitious pols, and some simply trying to find a way to get by. And through the days of the trial, the courtroom echoed with a wide range of sentiments and ideas, from appeals to civic pride, to the embrace of national values, to theories about criminal law and justice being debated in Europe.

But notwithstanding all this, from start to finish this had been a community matter with a distinctively local frame of reference.

Deliberately so. At the turn of the century, criminal justice systems in the Midwest, particularly in rapidly growing cities such as Chicago, were being pulled in two directions by equally strong forces. Proponents of law and order urged reform and the strengthening of the legal system, often arguing that changes were needed in the face of an uptick in immigration from countries, like Italy, not known for their devotion to the rule of law. Only a strong legal system would, these proponents urged, protect the community from the disorder that seemed close at hand. At the same time, the ideal of popular justice still had a strong pull, and its proponents struggled to keep control over defining crime and penalizing offenses in the hands of the people. They demanded the right of communities to participate actively in the capture of criminals and the punishing of crimes, they wanted crime and punishment to reflect local norms, and they insisted that transgressors be punished quickly and severely. As important, they often defined wrongdoing in communal terms, punishing most harshly those offenses that seemed to them the most dangerous to the community's well being.

As this suggests, the two opposing sides shared a point in common—the idea of community, which suggested a way to split the difference. The community could be brought into the criminal justice system. During the investigation of crimes, the community's proxies—the newspapers—could be part of police investigations and could also pressure the police to value the quick resolution of crimes over regulation. At trial, another set of proxies—members of the jury—could bring their common sense to bear, aided by judges and government officials who deferred to their judgment and valued their sense above the commands of law. In the process, trials became a referendum on community in another way as well, as juries punished outsiders who seemed the most threatening to the community order. Sometimes, as seemed to be the case in the Trunk Murder trial, the sense that the defendants represented a larger threat to the community—in this case, the entering wedge of the Mediterranean vendetta—led to convictions that were out of proportion to other, similar crimes. At other times, when jurors sensed that outsiders' criminality was directed toward their compatriots, they might rule leniently or acquit.

So some law-and-order reformers such as Hawes, and like the editorial board of the *Chicago Tribune*, adopted the idea of common-sense justice. And while their influence gave it a toehold, the process became self-reinforcing. Trials became a crapshoot, which, as Pound noted, only deepened the popular contempt for law. As Pound also noted, when judges and politicians ignored the law and winked at those who rose above it, this encouraged the police—already pressured by the press—to favor results and pragmatic solutions, even corrupt ones, over regulations. In this milieu it did not really matter if Azari, Gelardi, or Silvestri actually killed Filippo Caruso. What mattered was solving the mystery promptly and quickly convicting some people for the crime. And this is precisely what happened.

The Italians and Their Culture

Italians in the Trunk Murder Case

The complicated relationships among the various defendants and others involved in this case make it helpful to have some brief biographies that set out these connections. In the pages below, I have tried to supply the relevant details, as best as I have been able to reconstruct them from a variety of sources. The biographies are in alphabetical order. I have used the names found in the Italian records (although so there should be no confusion, I have placed the names used in this study in parentheses).[1]

GIOVANNI AZZARA (GIOVANNI AZARI)

Azzara was born in Sicily in approximately 1854, in Trabia, a small coastal town between Palermo and Termini Imerese. He trained as a shoemaker and in 1877 married Salvadora (or Salvatora) Demma, from Termini Imerese. They had three children: Crocifissa (1883–1883), Maria (born 1884), and Francesco (born 1885). He was not directly related to any of the defendants or the Carusos, though members of his wife's family had married Carusos and members of the Bova-Conti families in previous generations. Azzara took the *Archimede* steamship to New York in 1884, arriving on October 24. Agostino Gelardi was also on this ship. Azzara did not go straight to Chicago with Gelardi. Instead he apparently worked on a ship for the first several weeks after he arrived in the United States. Then in December 1884 he gave up that work and moved to Chicago. It appears that he moved in with some or all of the other defendants at this point, perhaps as a result of the connections he made with Gelardi on the *Archimede*. While in Chicago, Azzara joined the others in selling fruit, though he occasionally may have repaired shoes as well. Azzara was buried in Calvary Catholic Cemetery, in Chicago, under the name Giovanni Azari.

IGNAZIO BOVA-CONTI (IGNAZIO BOVA)

Ignazio Francesco Bova-Conti was born in Termini Imerese in 1858. As a young man he worked as a farmer and was not married. His family seems to have used the names Bova and Bova-Conti interchangeably; the Italian records inconsistently use either name for the same person or for members of the same family. His mother, Giuseppa Silvestre, was sister to Agostino Gelardi's mother, Maria Silvestre, and to Ignazio Silvestre's father, Francesco Agostino Silvestre. So Bova-Conti was first cousin to both Agostino Gelardi and Ignazio Silvestre. Ignazio Bova-Conti's uncle, Michele Salvadore Bova-Conti, was the man referred to as Mercurio's godfather. I have been unable to determine what happened to Bova-Conti after he was acquitted of Caruso's murder.

MICHELE SALVADORE BOVA-CONTI (SALVADORE BOVA-CONTI)

Michele Salvadore Bova-Conti, born in Termini Imerese in 1831, was a younger brother of Ignazio Bova-Conti's father, Agostino (born in 1821). He was, apparently, Antonino Mercurio's godfather and the man that Mercurio claimed to live with on Tilden Avenue. He was also the father of Salvadore Bova-Conti, aged approximately thirty in 1885, who sailed to New York with Ignazio Bova-Conti and Ignazio Silvestre in December 1884.

PASQUALE BOVA-CONTI

Pasquale Bova-Conti was born in Termini Imerese in 1855. His sister, Agata, was married to Antonio Mercurio. He was also Ignazio Silvestre's brother-in-law since his wife, Antonina, was the sister of Silvestre's wife, Antonia. It is unclear when Pasquale came to the United States, but Francesco Caruso's testimony suggests he was living with the Caruso brothers at 73 Tilden Avenue before Filippo's death and he was still living on Tilden Avenue when Azzara, Gelardi, and Silvestre were hanged.

ANTONINO CARUSO

Antonino Caruso, who was described in news accounts as Filippo Caruso's second cousin, was born in Termini Imerese in 1865. He worked as a laborer in Sicily and was unmarried when he sailed for the United States. He arrived in the port of New York on December 1, 1884, on the *Gottardo*, the same ship as Ignazio Bova-Conti and Ignazio Silvestre. He testified that he owned a grocery store in Chicago.

FILIPPO CARUSO

Filippo was born in Termini Imerese, Sicily, in 1859, to Francesco Caruso and Antonina Elisco. Francesco Caruso was his older brother. There is no record that Filippo was ever married; he worked as a laborer in Termini Imerese. Filippo Caruso was one of the first of the Sicilians involved in this case to arrive in the United States. He landed in New York in January 1884 and came to Chicago shortly thereafter. He lived with his brother Francesco and with Pasquale Bova-Conti at 73 Tilden Avenue, a building owned by Lorenz Ryder and his wife.

FRANCESCO CARUSO

Francesco Caruso, Filippo's older brother, was born in 1854 in Termini Imerese. He was a handyman (presumably a laborer) in Termini Imerese; there is no record that he ever married. He traveled to the United States on the *Indipendente*, landing in New York in March 1885. I have been unable to determine what happened to him after 1885.

AGOSTINO GELARDI

Gelardi was born in Termini Imerese, Sicily, in 1861. His mother, Maria Silvestre, was the sister of Francesco Silvestre (Ignazio Silvestre's father), and the sister of Guiseppa Silvestre, who married Agostino Bova-Conti and was mother of Ignazio Bova-Conti. So while Agostino Gelardi was cousin to Ignazio Silvestre and Ignazio Bova-Conti, the two Ignazios were not directly related to one another. Gelardi, a fisherman in Termini Imerese, was married to Maria Galluza. He traveled to the United States on the *Archimede*, the same ship that Giovanni Azzara sailed on, and landed in New York on October 24, 1884. He is buried in Calvary Catholic Cemetery in Chicago.

JOHN GINOCHIO

It is not entirely clear who the John Ginochio involved in the trial was. The 1880 census for Chicago listed two. One was twenty-seven and a notary public who lived on Madison; the other, John B. Ginochio, was forty-eight and was in the fruit and confectionary business. He lived on Halsted. The *Lakeside Directory, 1885*, lists two John Ginochios in Chicago. One is a partner in Daprato & Ginochio, a liquor store on 143 Halsted, which presumably means this is John B. Ginochio. The other was a salesman.

ANTONINO MERCURIO (ANTONIO MERCURIO)

Mercurio was born in Termini Imerese in 1844 and was the oldest of the defendants. In Sicily he was a fisherman. He married Agata Bova in 1868, and they had at least seven children. Five of those children were born before 1885; two were born afterward, which suggests that Mercurio returned to Termini Imerese after his acquittal. Mercurio was not directly related to any of the defendants or the Caruso brothers. However, Pasquale Bova-Conti, who lived with the Caruso brothers, was the brother of Mercurio's wife, Agata, and was Ignazio Silvestre's brother-in-law. Further, the man described as Mercurio's godfather, Salvadore Bova-Conti, was Ignazio Bova-Conti's uncle. Mercurio sailed to America on the *Indipendente* in June 1884. He claimed that, when he arrived in Chicago, he moved in with his godfather at 63 Tilden, but testimony during the trial suggested that he lived at 94 Tilden with the other defendants at the time of the murder.

MARINA MERCURIO

Marina Mercurio was Andrea Russo's wife. She was born in 1858 and married Russo in 1882. While her name suggests that she was related to Antonino Mercurio, I have been unable to determine how close the relationship was. She died in Chicago in 1924 and is buried in Calvary Cemetery.

JOSEPH OSTRELLA

According to the *Lakeside Directory, 1885*, Joseph Ostrella was a musician who lived at 1462 Wabash.

ANDREA RUSSO

Andrea Russo was born in Termini Imerese in approximately 1859. He arrived in Chicago with his wife in 1882. Russo stayed in Chicago and became a successful importer and an important figure in Chicago's Italian community. He died in a car crash in 1935. He was also buried in Calvary Catholic Cemetery.

IGNAZIO SILVESTRE (IGNAZIO SILVESTRI)

Ignazio Silvestre was born in 1862 and was a fisherman in Termini Imerese. He was first cousin to both Agostino Gelardi and Ignazio Bova-Conti. He was married in 1884 to Antonia Bova, the daughter of Salvatore Bova (or Bova-Lupo) and Giuseppa Giuliano. Pasquale Bova-Conti (who lived with the Caruso brothers on Tilden Avenue) was his brother-in-law because they were married to sisters. Silvestre traveled to America on the *Gottardo*, on the same passage as Ignazio Bova-Conti and Antonino Caruso. After his execution, Silvestre was buried at Calvary Cemetery in Chicago.

Italy and Sicily

There are any number of studies of nineteenth-century Italy and Sicily. For general overviews of Italian history, see Martin Clark, *Modern Italy, 1871–1982* (New York: Longman, 1984); John A. Davis, ed., *Italy in the Nineteenth Century, 1796–1900* (Oxford: Oxford University Press, 2000). The standard study of Sicilian history is Denis Mack Smith, *A History of Sicily: Modern Sicily after 1713* (London: Chatto and Windus, 1968). For more recent studies that consider Sicily in the context of the Risorgimento, see Lucy Riall, *Sicily and the Unification of Italy: Liberal Policy and Local Power* (New York: Oxford University Press, 1998), and Lucy Riall, "Elites in Search of Authority: Political Power and Social Order in Nineteenth-Century Sicily," *History Workshop Journal* 55 (2003): 25, 30–32. A number of recent articles and books have sketched the north–south divisions within Italy that followed the Risorgimento. For a sample, see Lucy Riall, "Garibaldi and the South," in Davis, *Italy in the Nineteenth Century*; Jane Schneider, ed., *Italy's "Southern Question": Orientalism in One Country* (New York: Berg, 1997); Nelson Moe, *The View from Vesuvius: Italian Culture and the Southern Question* (Berkeley and Los Angeles: University of California Press, 2002).

Italian Immigration

For studies of Italian immigration that focus on the immigration from southern Italy, see Donna R. Gabaccia, *From Sicily to Elizabeth Street: Housing and Social Change among Italian Immigrants, 1880–1930* (Albany: SUNY University Press, 1984), and Donna Rae Gabaccia, *Militants and Migrants: Rural Sicilians Become American Workers* (New Brunswick: Rutgers University Press, 1988). There are several studies that look at the experiences of Italians in turn-of-the-century Chicago. The first was a dissertation written by Rudolph Vecoli, "Chicago's Italians prior to World War I: A Study of Their Social and Economic Adjustment" (Ph.D. dissertation, University of Wisconsin, 1963). His work was further developed by Humbert S. Nelli, *Italians in Chicago, 1880–1930: A Study in Ethnic Mobility* (New York: Oxford University Press, 1970). There was also a major study of Italians in Chicago published by the Commissioner of Labor at the end of the nineteenth century; it gives a sense of employment opportunities and economic status. Commissioner of Labor, *The Italians in Chicago: A Social and Economic Study* (Washington, D.C., 1897).

Italian Language

The argument that the Sicilian language was very different from Italian was a major claim in the trial. For studies that support this argument, see Adam Ledgeway, *A Comparative Syntax of the Dialects of Southern Italy: A Minimalist Approach* (Oxford: Blackwell, 2000); H. H. Vaughn, "Studies in Italian Linguistics," *Italica* 13 (1936): 74; H. H. Vaughn, "The Implications of Dialect in Italy," *Italica* 3 (1928): 56. There are also brief discussions of the problems that the Sicilian language posed for those who spoke other dialects of Italian in Nelli, *Italians in Chicago*, 58 (congressional investigation hindered by lack of translators who understood Sicilian, and problems for "courts in cases involving immigrants"), and in John Dickie, *Cosa Nostra: A History of the Sicilian Mafia* (London: Hodder and Stoughton, 2004), 47 (Franchetti's problems understanding Sicilian). For discussions of the different dialects, and the issues they raised in Chicago in this period, see Vecoli, "Chicago's Italians," 57, 69–70, 80–81, 98, 165; Nelli, *Italians in Chicago*, 4–5, 36, 156–57. For an Italian–Sicilian dictionary that gives an idea of the differences in vocabulary in the late nineteenth century, see *Nuovo dizionario siciliano–italiano*, ed. Vincenzo Martillaro, 3rd ed. (1881; reprint, 1997).

The Mafia

Few subjects in Sicilian or immigration history are as contested as that of the Mafia, with scholars unable to agree on what it was or even whether it ever existed. Recent works tend to agree that there is, and was, a Mafia, though they disagree on how and why it arose. Franchetti's idea, discussed earlier in this book, that Sicilian lawlessness could be traced to the island's feudalism was echoed in some postwar work by Marxists. In reaction, another group of scholars led by Edward C. Banfield, picked up on another part of Franchetti's analysis and argued that the Mafia could exist because Sicilian society had destroyed any sense of shared moral values. Edward C. Banfield, *The Moral Basis of a Backward Society* (New York: Free Press, 1967). More recently, Robert Putnam echoed Franchetti and the Marxists when he argued that Sicilian amorality could be blamed on centuries of government failure. Robert D. Putnam, *Making Democracy Work: Civic Traditions in Modern Italy* (Princeton: Princeton University Press, 1994). Like Franchetti, Putnam laid blame on local government. Another line of studies has argued that the rise of the Mafia in Sicily reflected an adaptation to the pressures of a market economy. Anton Blok, *The Mafia of a Sicilian Village: A Study of Violent Peasant Entrepreneurs* (New York: Waveland Press, 1974); Diego Gambetta, *The Sicilian Mafia: The Business of Private Protection* (Cambridge: Harvard University Press, 1993). For a more extensive, critical review of the literature, see Jane C. Schneider and Peter T. Schneider, *Reversible Destiny: Mafia, Anti-Mafia, and the Struggle for Palermo* (Berkeley and Los Angeles: University of California Press, 2003).

Awareness of the Mafia in the United States is usually tied to the murder of the New Orleans police chief in 1890. Richard Gambino, *Vendetta* (Garden City: Doubleday, 1977); David Critchley, *The Origins of Organized Crime in America: The New York City Mafia, 1891–1931* (New York: Routledge, 2009). But there were accounts of the Mafia before that killing. See Citali Seton, "The Secret Societies of Southern Italy: The Camorra, Feudalism and Brigandage, the Mafia," *Lippincott's Magazine of Popular Literature and Science* 143 (1879): 579; "The Psychology of Murder," *International Review* 3 (January 1876): 73, 88–90 (discussing the Sicilian "Maffia"). And the New York police department did decide that a murder at the end of the 1880s was the work of "Mafia assassins." See *Chicago Tribune* articles, "Avengers of the Mafia," October 22, 1888, 5; "Secrets of the Mafia," October 23, 1888, 3; and "Organized for Crime," October 29, 1888, 3. For articles debating whether the Mafia had come to Chicago, see "The Murderous Mafia," *Daily Inter Ocean*, October 24, 1888, 8 (no Mafia in Chicago); "Has Chicago a Mafia," *Chicago Tribune*, October 24, 1888, 1 (yes). But see "Letter to the Editor," *Chicago Tribune*, October 26, 1888, 9 (rejecting the *Tribune*'s conclusion).

Two quick notes: A body in a trunk with its arms and legs bound is something of a cliché in material on the Mafia, but it is not clear that either meant anything, since other turn-of-the-century murderers put bodies into trunks. See, for example, Mary Ting Yi Lui, *The Chinatown Trunk Mystery: Murder, Miscegenation, and Other Dangerous Encounters in Turn-of-the-Century New York City* (Princeton: Princeton University Press, 2005). So too, while the description of how the body in trunk no. 4171 was bound sounds like the notorious Mafia technique *incaprettamento*, there were differences. The body in the Trunk Murder case had its arms and legs tied in front of the body, while in *incaprettamento* the arms and legs are typically tied behind the body. See V. Fineschi, A. S. Dell'Erba, M. D. Paolo, and P. Pocaccianti, "Typical Homicide Ritual of the Italian Mafia (Incaprettamento)," *American Journal of Medical Pathology* 19 (1998): 87, fig. 1 (demonstrating the position of the body in *incaprettamento*). Although this article suggests that *incaprettamento* had a symbolic or ritualistic value, one scholar has argued that statements by Mafia informers make it clear the technique was used because it was a convenient way of bundling up bodies. Alexander Stille, *Excellent Cadavers: The Mafia and the Death of the First Italian Republic* (New York: Vintage Press, 1995).

The Law

The Lawyers in the Case

Background material on several of the lawyers (everyone but Maurice Baumann and Kate Kane) can be found in *Bench and Bar in Chicago: Biographical Sketches* (Chicago, 1883).

MAURICE BAUMANN

The information on Maurice Baumann and his career is sparse. There is a brief biography of him in I. C. Harris, comp., *Colored Men's Professional and Business Directory of Chicago* (1886), 25. He is referred to in another turn-of-the-century study of African American lawyers: James H. Bradwell, "The Colored Bar in Chicago," *Michigan Law Review* 5 (1896): 385, 390. He appears, briefly, in Christopher Robert Reed, *Black Chicago's First Century, 1833–1900* (Columbia: University of Missouri Press, 2005), 264–65, which lists Baumann and some of Chicago's other black lawyers in the late nineteenth century; and in J. Clay Smith, *Emancipation: The Making of the Black Lawyer, 1844–1944* (Philadelphia: University of Pennsylvania Press, 1993), 160–61 (Baumann admitted to the bar in Rhode Island in 1877).

More could be done. Various news accounts, for example, hint at his interests and activities. See *Chicago Tribune* articles "John Brown League," September 23, 1891, 3 (Baumann the first president); and "The

Lake Wards," September 5, 1889, 5 (Bauman's letter to others in these wards, urging political reforms and appealing to historical analogies to support his arguments); also *Chicago Tribune* articles that suggest the areas of his practice, which seemed mostly to involve real estate, divorce work, and some employment-related areas: "Circuit Court—New Suits," November 6, 1892, 14 (Baumann the attorney of record in the Finley divorce case); and "Circuit Court—New Suits," December 20, 1892, 14 (Baumann the attorney of record in a suit against Poppenberg & Christenson Bros.).

DANIEL DONAHOE

After he graduated from Notre Dame Law School, Daniel Donahoe moved to Chicago and became a famous criminal defense lawyer. "Romantic Story of Notre Dame," *Chicago Tribune*, June 23, 1899, 43 (graduates of Notre Dame's law school). He played an active role in the reform branch of Chicago's Democratic Party; see "Political Meetings Today," *Chicago Tribune*, November 2, 1898, 3 (Donahoe and Altgeld speak at a Tenth Ward meeting at Novotny's Hall), but he does not seem to have sought public office. He worked on a number of famous cases over his career, the most famous being the notorious Cronin Murder case, a trial that involved charges of international terrorism, corruption in the Chicago Police Department, and a mysterious death. Elizabeth Dale, "*People v. Coughlin* and Criticisms of the Criminal Jury in Late Nineteenth-Century Chicago," *Northern Illinois Law Review* 28 (2008): 503.

PETER FOOTE

Although the decision to take the Trunk Murder suspects before the grand jury meant that police court judge Peter Foote never actually played a role in this case, his career as a police court judge provides some perspective on the lower echelons of criminal justice in Chicago. For a sample of the sorts of cases he heard, and problems he had running for office, see *Chicago Tribune* articles "Criminal," November 18, 1875, 8 (Foote in police court); "Local Politics," October 19, 1877, 5 (Foote as candidate under Greenbacker Ticket); "Condit's Case," March 16, 1878, 3 (dismissing bribery case on ex post facto grounds); "A Test Case," November 27, 1879, 6 (Foote's suit against Chicago); "The Justices," April 17, 1879, 2 (opposition to Foote within the Democratic Party based on trumped-up charges by those who resent his reforming zeal); "Peter Foote," April 18, 1879, 6 (Foote a favorite of the "silk stocking" faction of the Democratic Party but is opposed by their opponents as a reformer); "Gossip," March 16, 1883, 6 (Foote opposed by the established Democratic Party in Chicago); "Editorial," March 20, 1883, 4 (hostility to Foote); Michael Willrich, *City of Courts: Socializing Justice in Progressive Era Chicago* (New York: Cambridge University Press, 2003), 14 (Foote taught at Notre Dame before becoming police court justice).

Much of the hostility toward Foote appeared to be caused by his reforming tendencies and iconoclastic personality, but Foote did seem to have more than his share of problems. See articles in the *Chicago Tribune*, "Alleged Illegal Fees," March 5, 1879, 8 (sued for collecting illegal fees); "Justice Foote," March 11, 1879, 8 (acquitted of charges of seeking illegal fees); "An Unfortunate Capitalist, and His Experience of the Law's Uncertainties," June 22, 1882, 16 (sued unsuccessfully in federal court, charged with fraud with respect to the purchase of a trust deed); "In General," May 15, 1884, 8 (Foote sued for an unpaid liquor bill of $50.00).

JULIUS GRINNELL

The most obvious sources for material on Grinnell are studies of the Haymarket trial, since it was the centerpiece of his career. Paul Avrich, *The Haymarket Tragedy* (Princeton: Princeton University Press, 1984); James R. Green, *Death in the Haymarket: A Story of Chicago, the First Labor Movement, and the Bombing that Divided Gilded Age America* (New York: Pantheon Books, 2006); Carl Smith, *Urban Disorder and the Shape of Disbelief: The Great Chicago Fire, the Haymarket Bomb, and the Model Town of Pullman* (2nd ed.; Chicago: University of Chicago Press, 2007). For Grinnell's work on the Boodler case, the large corruption trial that also helped launch his career, see the daily coverage in the Chicago papers from February 1887 through the verdict on June 19, 1887. McGarigle's attack on Grinnell during the case, Grinnell's response, McGarigle's flight from justice, and Grinnell's efforts to prosecute McGarigle are discussed in the following *Chicago Tribune* articles: "Desperate Boodlers," February 17, 1887, 1, 2 (McGarigle's complaint); "The Chicago Boodlers," March 17, 1887, 5 (McGarigle in custody); "The Boodlers Convicted," June 19, 1887, 1; "W. J. M'Garigle Escapes," June 24, 1887, 9; "M'Garigle Gets Off Easy," June 1, 1899, 4 (returns to Chicago to plead guilty and pay his fine). See also Flinn, *History of the Chicago Police*, 211–12

(McGarigle as superintendent of police).

For *Daily Inter Ocean* articles that fill in the details on Grinnell and his career, see "Special Bail," August 26, 1879, 2 (city attorney); "Hotel Bars," December 24, 1879, 3 (advises mayor he has the power to shut down hotel bars at midnight); "Wooden Signs," November 20, 1879, 8 (letter to the superintendent of buildings regarding the ordinance regulating sign size); "Democratic Primary Elections," March 26, 1881, 2 (won nomination for city attorney again). Grinnell's political ambitions are sketched out in "A Possible Mayor," January 15, 1891, 5 (somewhat jaundiced article on his political career by a Republican paper that had endorsed him after the Haymarket trial), and he became a judge after the Haymarket trial. Finally, see "Jurist Dies Suddenly," *Milwaukee Journal*, June 8, 1898, 6.

KIRK HAWES

For contemporary descriptions of Hawes, see J. Seymour Currey, "Kirk Hawes," in *Chicago, Its History and Its Builders: A Century of Marvelous Growth* (Chicago: S. J. Clarke, 1912), 4:646; "Obituary: Kirk Hawes," *New York Times*, September 10, 1904, 9. His work as a reformer, and his efforts on behalf of John Thomas, the African American attorney, are described in David A. Joens, "John W. E. Thomas and the Election of the First African American to the Illinois General Assembly," *Journal of the Illinois Historical Society* 94 (2001): 200. For more details of Hawes's career, see "Republican Gatherings," *Chicago Tribune*, October, 3, 1875, 9 (speech to Fourth Ward Republicans); "Mr. Hawes Declines," *Chicago Tribune*, April 5, 1876, 2 (disclaims any interest in being city attorney); "Local: The First Congressional," *Chicago Tribune*, August 3, 1876, 1 (candidate to represent Chicago's First Congressional District); "Convention Notes," *New York Times*, June 14, 1876, 5 (role in that convention); *Daily Inter Ocean*, May 28, 1880, 4 (speech in opposition to Grant in the 1880 convention); "Kirk Hawes," *Chicago Tribune*, May 22, 1880, 3 (candidate for lieutenant governor); "Kirk Hawes," *Chicago Tribune*, September 25, 1880, 6 (running for judge in the 1880 election); "Lawyer's Meeting," *Chicago Times*, April 14, 1888, 1 (considering a run for governor); "Judge Hawes Accepts," *Daily Inter Ocean*, March 25, 1895, 12 (agrees to run a good government committee in Chicago's Second Ward); "Kirk Hawes Indorsed," *Daily Inter Ocean*, March 9, 1895, 8 (endorsed for alderman by Republicans); "Indorse Kirk Hawes," *Daily Inter Ocean*, March 13, 1895, 8 (endorsed for Second Ward alderman by Civic Foundation).

KATE KANE ROSSI

Recent studies of women who practiced law at the turn of the century often discuss Kane's career. See, for example, The Women's Legal History Website, maintained by Stanford University (www.law.stanford. edu/library/womenslegalhistory) (entry under Kate Kane) and Gwen Hoerr McNamee, ed., *Bar None: 125 Years of Women Lawyers in Illinois* (Chicago: Chicago Bar Association Alliance for Women, 1998). Kane was also the subject of some contemporary studies; see Leila J. Robinson, "Women Lawyers in the United States," *Green Bag* 2 (1890): 10.

Kane was frequently in the news, which means that there are quite a few articles describing the nature and extent of her activism. For a sample, see "Obituary: Kate Kane Rossi," *Chicago Tribune*, November 23, 1928, 22 (studied law at the University of Michigan); "Kate Kane's Hobby," *Milwaukee Daily Sentinel*, January 1881, 8 (call for the hiring of matrons); "Debut of Miss Kate Kane as a Platform Speaker," *Milwaukee Daily Sentinel*, February 25, 1881, 3 (speech on economic injustice); "Kate Kane," *Milwaukee Daily Sentinel*, March 29, 1881, 9 (protesting the fact women lacked the franchise); "Kate Kane at Eau Claire," *Milwaukee Daily Sentinel*, July 28, 1881, 7 (speech on economic injustice and the need for strikes to advance the rights of the poor); "Letter to the Editor," *Milwaukee Daily Sentinel*, February 27, 1883, 8 (support for the work of the YMCA to help prisoners); "Kate Kane in War-paint," *Milwaukee Daily Journal*, January 4, 1883, 8 (judge referred to two women as sluts, Kane protested); "Letter to the Editor," *Milwaukee Daily Journal*, January 8, 1883, 2 (judges and attorneys in a courtroom mocked her and other women in their absence, Kane protested). Throughout her career as an activist, Kane mounted symbolic campaigns for public office. See, for example, "Kate Kane Will Run for Judge," *Boston Daily Advertiser*, July 21, 1893, 5 (announcing her candidacy); "Kate Kane Still Talks," *Milwaukee Daily Journal*, December 21, 1895, 5 (against the degraded position of women); "Woman Seeks Police Headship," *Christian Science Monitor*, April 15, 1911, 5 (presents self-nomination to Chicago's mayor).

Her contempt case is set out in the following series of articles: "A Pint of Water," *Milwaukee Daily Journal*, April 21, 1883, 3 (contempt of court); "Kate Kane's Kase," *Milwaukee Daily Sentinel*, April 22, 1883, 3 (petition for writ of habeas corpus); "After Kate Kane," *Milwaukee Daily Journal*, April 23, 1883, 3 (attorneys seek to have her rearrested); "Editorial," *Milwaukee Sentinel*, April 24, 1883, 2 (quoting the editor of the *Democrat*); "Kate Kane Held," *Milwaukee Daily Journal*, April 30,

1883, 3; *Milwaukee Daily Sentinel,* May 24, 1883, 4 (released four days earlier); "Kate Kane Presented with a Purse by Her Friends," *Milwaukee Daily Sentinel,* May 20, 1883, 4 (letter signed by one hundred women in Milwaukee); "Kate Kane on Deck," *Milwaukee Daily Journal,* September 14, 1883, 4 (problems resuming her practice). And this was not the end of her problems practicing. See "Kate Kane Shabbily Treated," *Milwaukee Daily Sentinel,* January 27, 1884, 4 (problems with attorneys at a trial in Chicago, coincidentally before Judge Kirk Hawes).

NATHANIEL SEARS

There is strikingly little material on Sears. Other than the brief entry on his firm in the *Bench and Bar,* the most detail about his life is provided in "Judge Sears' Home Life," *Chicago Tribune,* March 1, 1897, 9. The following *Chicago Tribune* articles suggest his legal career: "The Bar Association," April 7, 1878, 8 (membership in the association); "Mr. Goudy Is Silent," August 22, 1892, 6 (candidacy for a judicial position and endorsements); "Labor's Great Day," September 4, 1892, 11 (speaker at the Labor Day celebration in Chicago); "Gary at its Head," October 7, 1893, 9 (nominated for judge by the Republican Party); "Hero of All Ages," February 23, 1894, 1 (attends Washington Birthday celebration).

Criminal Law and Rough Justice

CRIMINAL JUSTICE AT THE TURN OF THE CENTURY

There are several overviews of criminal law and practice in the United States, including Lawrence M. Friedman, *Crime and Punishment in American History* (New York: Basic Books, 1993); Samuel Walker, *Popular Justice: A History of American Criminal Justice* (2nd ed.; New York: Oxford University Press, 1998). In addition, the subject is treated in Kermit Hall and Peter Karsten, *The Magic Mirror: Law in American History* (2nd ed.; New York: Oxford University Press, 2009); Lawrence M. Friedman, *American Law in the Twentieth Century* (New Haven: Yale University Press, 2002); and Lawrence M. Friedman, *A History of American Law,* 3rd ed. (New York: Touchstone, 2005). For two recent articles that put turn-of-the-century criminal law into its larger, longer contexts, see Elizabeth Dale, "Criminal Justice in the United States, 1790–1920," in *Cambridge History of Law in America: The Long Nineteenth Century,* ed. Christopher Tomlins and Michael Grossberg

(New York: Cambridge University Press, 2008), 2: 133-67; and Michael Willrich, "Criminal Justice in the United States," in *Cambridge History of Law in America: The Twentieth Century and After*, 3: 195–231.

For a survey of crime and punishment in Chicago at the turn of the century, see John H. Wigmore, ed., *The 1929 Illinois Crime Survey* (Chicago: Illinois Association for Criminal Justice, 1929). There are also a number of historical studies that look at aspects of criminal justice in turn-of-the-century Chicago. See Richard Schneirov, *Labor and Urban Politics: Class Conflict and the Origins of Modern Liberalism in Chicago, 1864–1897* (Urbana: University of Illinois Press, 1998); Elizabeth Dale, *The Rule of Justice: The People of Chicago versus Zephyr Davis* (Columbus: Ohio State University Press, 2001); Willrich, *City of Courts*; David Tanenhaus, *Juvenile Justice in the Making* (New York: Oxford University Press, 2004); Jeffrey S. Adler, *First in Violence, Deepest in Dirt: Homicide in Chicago, 1875–1920* (Cambridge: Harvard University Press, 2006); and Carl Smith, *Urban Disorder and the Shape of Disbelief* (2nd ed.; Chicago: University of Chicago Press, 2007).

ROUGH JUSTICE

A number of recent works have traced out the tangled relationship between informal processes of judging and punishing and the formal system of criminal law, a dynamic that had its roots in the colonial era. The starting point for studies of rough justice is Richard Maxwell Brown, *Strain of Violence: Historical Studies of American Violence and Vigilantism* (New York: Oxford University Press, 1975). Laura Edwards explores the close relationship between popular justice and formal law and explains how and why they came to be split apart during the antebellum era in *The People and Their Peace: Legal Culture and the Transformation of Inequality in the Post-Revolutionary South* (Chapel Hill: University of North Carolina Press, 2009). I sketch the relationship between antebellum rough justice and other sorts of popular justice in Elizabeth Dale, "Popular Sovereignty: A Case Study from the Antebellum Era," in *Constitutional Mythologies: New Perspectives on Controlling the State*, ed. Alain Marciano (New York: Springer, forthcoming); Elizabeth Dale, "A Different Sort of Justice: The Informal Courts of Public Opinion in Antebellum South Carolina," *South Carolina Law Review* 54 (2003): 627.

Christopher Waldrep traces the evolution of rough justice across the nineteenth century in *Roots of Disorder: Race and Criminal Justice in the American South* (Urbana: University of Illinois Press, 1998). For the two major studies that look at the struggle between rough justice and proponents of the rule of law in the decades after the Civil War, see W. Fitzhugh Brundage, *Lynching in the New South: Georgia and Virginia, 1880–1930* (Urbana: University of Illinois Press, 1993), and Michael J. Pfeifer, *Rough Justice: Lynching and American Society, 1874–1947* (Urbana: University of Illinois Press, 2006). While Waldrep, Brundage, and Pfeifer look at the violent forms taken by rough justice between the Civil War and 1930, I look at some of the softer forms of popular justice (mobbing, ignoring the law, jury nullification) and their impact on the courts; see Dale, *Rule of Justice*; Elizabeth Dale, "Not Simply Black and White: Jury Power in the Late Nineteenth Century," *Social Science History* 25 (2001): 7; Elizabeth Dale, "'Social Equality Does Not Exist among Themselves, nor among Us': *Baylies v. Curry* and Civil Rights in Chicago, 1888," *American Historical Review* 107 (1997): 311. While those studies suggest that popular or rough justice was a uniquely American phenomenon, this was obviously not the case. For an article that sketches the international or transnational context of the rough justice debates, see Anna di Bobiant, "Genealogy of Soft Law," *American Journal of Comparative Law* 54 (2006): 499.

These scholarly works on rough justice rest on news accounts of lynchings and vendettas from around the United States. For just some of the articles, suggesting the scope of rough justice at the turn of the century, see the following.

The South—"Sad Sequence of the Louisiana Vendetta," *Daily Cleveland Herald*, May 9, 1870, 2 (vendetta in Catahoula, Louisiana); "The Feud of Blood," *Daily Cleveland Herald*, August 5, 1870, 2 (Shelby County, Tennessee); "From Barnwell," *Charleston Courier*, October 27, 1870, 1 (Barnwell County, South Carolina); "A Virginia Vendetta," *Daily Evening Bulletin*, October 16, 1872, 8 (son avenges father in Virginia); "The Murdered Ferryman," *Little Rock Daily Republican*, May 4, 1874, 2 (vendetta death in Little Rock, Arkansas); "A Texas Vendetta," *Daily Inter Ocean*, June 27, 1874, 2 (vendetta death in Galveston, Texas); "A Garrulous Man's Story," *San Francisco Daily Evening Bulletin*, May 8, 1875, 4 (vendetta in Tallahassee, Florida); "Baldwin County (Alabama) Vendetta," *Galveston Daily News*, July 30, 1875, 2 (vendetta murder near Mobile, Alabama); "A Kentucky Vendetta," *Boston Daily Advertiser*, December 27, 1877, 2 (twenty-three-year war between two families); "A South Carolina Battle," *Galveston Daily News*, August 14, 1878, 3 (feud in Edgefield, South Carolina, leads to more deaths); "A Texas

Vendetta," *St. Louis Globe-Democrat*, May 12, 1879, 7 (recent deaths in a feud between two families in Hempstead, Texas); "A Kentucky Vendetta," *Galveston Daily News*, May 27, 1879, 3 (recent deaths in feud between families in Castor County, Kentucky); "Carter County Vendetta," *St. Louis Globe-Democrat*, October 15, 1879, 4 (feud resumed in Kentucky); "A War Vendetta," *Milwaukee Sentinel*, January 15, 1883, 6 (family feud in Texas and Arkansas); "A Bloody Vendetta," *Little Rock Daily Arkansas Gazette*, May 22, 1883, 2 (killings of several members of one family by members of another near Baton Rouge, Louisiana); "Calendar of Crime," *St. Louis Globe-Democrat*, May 29, 1883, 6 (father and son killed as part of family feud in Tennessee); "Criminal Calendar," *St. Louis Globe-Democrat*, January 8, 1884, 3 (feud between two families in Shelby, North Carolina, leads to murder).

North and Middle West—"A Sad Story," *San Francisco Daily Evening Bulletin*, April 18, 1873, 10 (in New York City); "The Moody-Tolliver Vendetta," *San Francisco Daily Evening Bulletin*, April 28, 1874, 2 (feud in Lawrence County, Indiana); "A Village Vendetta," *Milwaukee Daily Sentinel*, July 16, 1874, 8 (vendetta killing by Lake Creek in Wisconsin); "An Illinois Vendetta," *Milwaukee Sentinel*, December 23, 1874, 7 (feud killings near Cairo, Illinois); "The Warren County (Iowa) Vendetta," *Daily Inter Ocean*, February 24, 1876, 8 (vendetta killings in Iowa); "The Warren County (Iowa) Vendetta," *Daily Inter Ocean*, February 24, 1876, 8 (vendetta killings in Iowa); "The Newark Vendetta," *Milwaukee Daily Sentinel*, July 17, 1876, 7 (deaths in New Jersey resemble accounts of vendettas from the West); "A Black Vendetta," *Daily Inter Ocean*, July 9, 1879, 3 (vendetta within the Jones family); "An Indiana Vendetta," *Little Rock Daily Arkansas Gazette*, September 1, 1880, 1 (decades-long feud in Indiana prompts a shooting Danville).

The West—"A Vendetta in Mendocino County," *San Francisco Daily Evening Bulletin*, August 30, 1877, 2 (feud between two families in California lead to deaths); "A Bloody Vendetta Occurs at Buena Vista," *Daily Rocky Mountain News*, August 15, 1880, 3 (several killed in revenge killing in California); "Vendetta in Arizona," *San Francisco Daily Evening Bulletin*, March 23, 1882, 3 (murder as a part of campaign of assassinations in Arizona Territory); "A Vendetta," *Weekly Los Angeles Mirror*, July 11, 1885, 3 (feud in San Luis Obispo leads to several killings); "A Shoshone Vendetta," *St. Louis Globe-Democrat*, November 8, 1885, 6 (suspicion of adultery leads to vendetta and several deaths in Wyoming).

Criminology and Criminal Anthropology

The turn of the century was also a period of rich theorizing about crime and criminality. For some examples of the century's discussions of criminals and criminal law, see Charles Loring Brace, *The Dangerous Classes of New York and Twenty Years among Them* (New York, 1872); Richard Dugdale, *The Jukes: A Study in Crime, Pauperism, Disease and Heredity* (New York, 1877); H. L. Wayland, "Social Science in the Laws of Moses: Wages and Pledges, Dignity of Labor, Crime, Humanity," *Journal of Social Sciences* 23 (1883): 167.

Italy was a leader in the field of criminal anthropology at the turn of the century, and Italian theories of criminality, particularly Cesare Lombroso's *L'uomo deliquente* (1876), seemed to influence Baumann's closing argument in the Trunk Murder trial. On Lombroso, see Mary Gibson, *Born to Crime: Cesare Lombroso and the Origins of Biological Criminality* (Westport, Conn.: Praeger, 2002), 21–22. As Gibson notes, Lombroso's theories evolved over time, but in their earliest manifestation he emphasized the physiological causes of crime, arguing that criminals could be identified by their "abnormal anatomical and biological traits" (Gibson, *Born to Crime*, 22). Gibson's book discusses when, and how, Lombroso's work became influential in the United States (22). The earliest discussion of Lombroso I have been able to locate is by Emile de Leveleye: "Professor Lombroso, in his curious work 'L'Uomo Delinquente,' explains that criminals' instinct and nature act the same way, and they are wholly different from those who may be called 'chance' criminals." Emile de Leveleye, "Pessimism on the Stage," *Eclectic Magazine of Foreign Literature* 42 (1885): 537, 542 (quote). See a brief mention of Lombroso and the Italian positivists in "Note," *Harvard Law Review* 3 (1889–1890): 280; and the Italian school of criminology, especially Garofalo, in "Review: *The Criminal* by Havelock Ellis," *Juridical Review* 2 (1890): 381; also "Review: *La Criminologie*," *Juridical Review* 3 (1890): 161; Helen Zimmers, "Criminal Anthropology in Italy," *Green Bag* 10 (1898): 382; Gino Speranza, "Lombroso in Science and Fiction," *Green Bag* 13 (1901): 122. For the impact those theories had, particularly on immigrant and minority defendants, see generally Gibson, *Born to Crime*, 44–45; Peter d'Agostino, "Craniums, Criminals and the 'Cursed Race': Italian Anthropology in American Racial Thought, 1861–1924," *Comparative Studies in History and Sociology* 44 (2002): 319.

Lombroso's argument resembled a theory that had been made in the United States by Richard Dugdale in *The Jukes*. Modern scholars often lump Dugdale and Lombroso together as Social Darwinists or proponents of a theory of atavistic criminality; see, for example, Cara W. Boinson, "Representing 'Miss Lizzie': Cultural Convictions in the Trial of Lizzie Borden," *Yale Journal of Law & Humanities* 8 (1996): 351, 377; Herbert Hoverkamp, "Evolutionary Models in Jurisprudence," *Texas Law Review* 64 (1985): 645, 684n212. On the other hand, commentators in the late nineteenth century tended to draw distinctions between the two, seeing a stronger environmental element in Dugdale's work. See, for example, *The Nation* 47 (August 9, 1888): 102. Nicole Hahn Rafter captured this distinction in noting Dugdale asserted that environmental changes such as good health and moral improvement could turn even the born criminal from a life of crime, while Lombroso inclined toward biological determinism—one born a criminal would die a criminal and give birth to criminals. Nicole Hahn Rafter, "Seeing and Believing: Images of Heredity in Biological Theories of Crime," *Brooklyn Law Review* 6 (2001): 71, 84.

Police at the Turn of the Century

• The general rules of late nineteenth-century police investigations are set out in Robert H. Vickers, *The Powers and Duties of Police Officers and Coroners* (Chicago, 1889). An extremely rosy picture of the Chicago Police Department at the turn of the century is set out in John Joseph Flinn, *History of the Chicago Police Department* (1887; reprint ed., New York: AMS Press, 1973); another is Michael Schaack, *Anarchy and Anarchists* (1889; reprint, New York: Arno Press, 1977), a study of the police department's investigation of the Haymarket case, written by Michael Schaack, one of the officers in charge of the case. A considerably darker picture emerges in John H. Wigmore, ed., *The 1929 Illinois Crime Survey* (Chicago: Illinois Association for Criminal Justice, 1929), esp. ch. 8, which looks specifically at the Chicago Police Department; and Richard Lindberg, *To Serve and Collect: Chicago Politics and Police Corruption from the Lager Beer Riot to the Summerdale Scandal* (New York: Praeger, 1991).

There were several investigations into the Chicago Police Department around the turn of the century. Illinois General Assembly, *Senate Report on the Chicago Police System* (Springfield, Ill.: Phillips Bros, 1898); Chicago Civil Service Commission, *Final Report, Police Investigation* (Chicago, 1912); Citizens' Police Committee, *Chicago Police Problems* (Chicago: University of Chicago Press, 1931). In addition, Chicago's police were a constant target of stories in Chicago's newspapers. Twice in the 1880s (in 1885 and again in 1889), Chicago papers published extended series charging corruption in the force. For

Chicago Daily News articles in the 1885 series reporting the investigation into misconduct in Bonfield's district, see "An Appalling Revelation," September 22, 1885, 1; "Revelation Number Two," September 24, 1885, 1; "Revelation Number Three," September 26, 1885, 1; "Gambling Not Stopped," September 26, 1885, 2; "Result of the Exposure," September 30, 1885, 1; "Captain Bonfield's Defense," October 5, 1885, 2; "Toughdom's Stronghold," October 31, 1885, 1.

For the *Chicago Times* 1889 series, focused particularly on Bonfield's district, see "A Terrible Lesson," January 28, 1889, 1 (foreign-born machine-shop owner who complained of theft harassed by the police); "Typical Police Methods," January 30, 1889, 1 (foreign-born delivery-wagon owner harassed); "It Looks Suspicious," January 10, 1889, 1 (lawyer charges that Bonfield helped a witness disappear); "Bonfield's Crooked Work," January 10, 1889, 2 (Bonfield interfered with a murder case and hindered an investigator who was not his ally); "Captain Hathaway's Revenge," January 17, 1889, 1 (attack on a political opponent); "Schaak as Whitewasher," January 19, 1889, 1 (Bonfield helps Schaak cover up misconduct); "Builders Shaken Down by Police," January 21, 1889, 1 (builders forced to make deals with police in order to avoid citations and complaints about their work); "More Police Peculiarities," January 21, 1889, 1 (when the jail needs repairs the police make arrests of workers with the necessary skills).

Bonfield's conduct during the Haymarket investigation was praised in Michael Schaack, *Anarchy and Anarchists* (1889; reprint, New York: Arno Press, 1977) and condemned by John Peter Altgeld, *The Chicago Martyrs: Reasons for Pardoning Fielden, Neebe, and Schwab* (1899; reprint, Chicago: Charles H. Kerr, 1986). Historians tend to agree with Altgeld; see Avrich, *Haymarket Tragedy*; Green, *Death in the Haymarket*; Smith, *Urban Disorder and the Shape of Disbelief.*

The *Chicago Tribune* was Bonfield's staunchest advocate, especially in the years following Haymarket, and was quick to leap to his defense. See "Ridiculous Stories about the Detective Bureau," April 22, 1888, 28; "A Tribute to Bonfield," January 6, 1889, 9 (letter to the editor in praise of Bonfield); "Editorial," February 3, 1889, 4 (Tuley's ruling would interfere with effective police techniques); "Criminals Grow Bold," February 6, 1889, 3 (Tuley's ruling encouraged criminals to flout the law). But not everyone was convinced.

Turn-of-the-century Chicago was not unique in its problems of police corruption or misconduct. For police departments, corruption, and efforts at reform in general, see Eric Monkkonen, *Police in Urban America, 1860–1920* (New York: Cambridge University Press,

2004). For a contemporary overview of the problem, see the Wickersham Commission's exposé of turn-of-the-century police misconduct, published as a report in 1931. National Commission on Law Observance and Enforcement [the Wickersham Commission], *Report on Lawlessness in Law Enforcement*. Washington, D.C.: Government Printing Office, 1931. There is a rich literature on police corruption in different parts of the country; see Warren Sloat, *A Battle for the Soul of New York: Tammany Hall, Police Corruption, Vice, and the Reverend Charles Parkhurst's Crusade against Them, 1892–1895* (New York: Copper Square, 2002); Jesse T. Todd, Jr., "Battling Satan in the City: Charles Henry Parkhurst and Municipal Redemption in Gilded Age New York," *American Presbyterians* 71 (1993): 243; Eugene J. Watts, "The Police in Atlanta," *Journal of Southern History* 39 (1973): 165; Elliott West, "Cleansing the Queen City: Prohibition and Urban Reform in Denver," *Arizona and the West* 14 (1972): 331 (lax police enforcement of anti-gambling and vice laws tied to corruption in Denver).

Another target of reform efforts at the turn of the century was police brutality: "The 'third degree' has become an every day feature of police investigation of crime." Roscoe Pound, "Law in Books and Law in Action," *American Law Review* 44 (1910): 12, 16; see also Wickersham Commission Report. Police misconduct and brutality affected immigrant and minority populations in particular. See Mario T. Garcia, "Porfirian Diplomacy and the Administration of Justice in Texas, 1877–1900," *Aztlan* 16 (1985): 1 (police brutality against Mexicans); George C. Wright, "The Billy Club and the Ballot: Police Intimidation of Blacks in Louisville, Kentucky, 1880–1930," *Southern Studies* 23 (1984): 20 (police brutality against blacks); J. William Snodgrass, "The Black Press in the San Francisco Bay Area, 1856–1900," *California History* 60 (1981–1982): 306 (newspaper campaign against police brutality); Gilbert Osofsky, "Race Riot, 1900: A Study of Ethnic Violence," *Journal of Negro Education* 32 (1964): 16, 22 (police brutality during class with blacks in Washington, D.C.).

Immigrants and Criminal Law

• Police were not the only source of problems for immigrants. Almost one hundred years ago, Grace Abbott published a study that looked at how immigrants were treated in the criminal courts of Chicago. Grace Abbott, "The Treatment of Aliens in the Criminal Court," *Journal of the American Institute of Criminal Law and Criminology* 2 (1912): 554. Sixty years later, David Colburn and George Pozzetta published an article that reviewed the field and argued far more had to be done to unpack the ways in which immigrants and members of minority groups experienced crime and criminal justice in the United States. David R. Colburn and George E. Pozzetta, "Crime and Ethnic Minorities in America: A Bibliographic Essay," *History Teacher* 7 (1974): 597. Since that article, historians have paid more attention to this issue, often looking at the experiences of members of particular ethnic or racial groups in specific regions. Mario T. Garcia, "Porfirian Diplomacy and the Administration of Justice in Texas, 1877–1900," *Aztlan* 16 (1985): 1; Vanessa Gunther, "Indians and the Criminal Justice System in San Bernardino and San Diego Counties, 1850–1900," *Journal of the West* 39 (2000): 26; Paul T. Hiettler, "A Surprising Amount of Justice: The Experience of Mexican and Racial Minority Defendants Charged with Serious Crimes in Arizona, 1865–1920," *Pacific Historical Review* 70 (2001): 193; John C. Lammers, "The Accommodation of Chinese Immigrants in Early California Courts," *Sociological Perspectives* 31 (1988): 446; Batya Miller, "Enforcement of the Sunday Closing Laws on the Lower East Side, 1820–1903," *American Jewish History* 91

(2003): 269; Khalil G. Muhammad, "Race, Crime, and Social Mobility: Black and Italian Undesirables in Modern America," *Proceedings of the American Italian Historical Association* 30 (1997): 172; Humbert S. Nelli, "Italians and Crime in Chicago: The Formative Years, 1890–1920," *American Journal of Sociology* 74 (1969); Gilbert Osofsky, "Race Riot, 1900: A Study of Ethnic Violence," *Journal of Negro Education* 32 (1964): 16; Linda S. Parker, "Statutory Changes and Ethnicity in Sex Crimes in Our California Counties, 1880–1920," *Western Legal History* 6 (1993): 69; Paul R. Spitzzeri, "On a Case-by-Case Basis: Ethnicity and Los Angeles Courts, 1850–1870," *California History* 83 (2005): 26; K. Scott Wong, "'The Eagle Seeks a Helpless Quarry': Chinatown, the Police, and the Press," *Amerasia Journal* 22 (1996): 81; George C. Wright, "The Billy Club and the Ballot: Police Intimidation of Blacks in Louisville, Kentucky, 1880–1930," *Southern Studies* 23 (1984): 20; Peter D'Agostino, "Craniums, Criminals, and the 'Cursed Race': Italian Anthropology in American Racial Thought, 1861–1924," *Comparative Studies in History and Society* 44 (2002): 319. Jeffrey Adler has looked at the variety of immigrants' experiences in Chicago criminal courts in *Deepest in Dirt*.

This is an area that calls out for comparative study, since studies of the experiences of immigrants or colonized peoples in Great Britain or in English common law courts provide an interesting contrast to the studies of those experiences in the United States. For a general overview focused on Great Britain, see Carolyn A. Conley, "Wars among Savages: Homicide and Ethnicity in the Victorian United Kingdom," *Journal of British Studies* 44 (2005): 775. For a recent study that looks at Chinese immigrants in Great Britain and offers a more critical perspective, see Sascha Auerbach, *Race, Law, and "The Chinese Puzzle" in Imperial Britain* (New York: Palgrave MacMillan, 2009). For other studies that look at the way due process worked—or failed to work—in Britain's colonial courts, see Kristyn Evelyn Harman, "Aboriginal Convicts: Race, Law, and Transportation in Colonial New South Wales" (Ph.D. dissertation, University of Tasmania, 2008); and Christopher Munn, "The Transportation of Chinese Convicts from Hong Kong, 1844–1858," *Journal of the Canadian Historical Association* 8 (1997): 113.

Auerbach's book deals with the problems that resulted from failing to provide interpreters for non-English-speaking immigrants, and several of the other studies of colonial courts discuss the adequacy of interpreters. For a contemporary account of interpreters in Chicago's criminal courts at the turn of the century, see Grace Abbott, "The Treatment of Aliens in the Criminal Court," *Journal of the American Institute of Criminal Law & Criminology* 2 (1912): 554.

Notes

Introduction

1. "A Gallows for Three," *Chicago Herald*, July 2, 1885, 1; "Three Lives for One," *Chicago Herald*, November 15, 1885, 9. On spectacular trials, see Michael A. Trotti, "The Lure of the Sensational Murder," *Journal of Social History* 35 (2001): 429.

2. Portions of this introduction were first printed as "It Makes Nothing Happen: Reasons for Studying the History of Law," *Law, Culture and Humanities* 5 (2009): 3. For some of the contemporary work rethinking originalism, see *Advance: The Journal of the ACS Issue Groups* 1 (Fall 2007), in particular the articles by Keith E. Whittington, Jack M. Balkin, and Kermit Roosevelt.

3. Robert Darnton, "It Happened One Night," *New York Review of Books* 51 (June 24, 2004): 60, 63–64. Darnton's incident analysis has much in common with what William Fisher characterized as New Historicism. William Fisher III, "Texts and Contexts: The Application to American Legal History of the Methodologies of Intellectual History," *Stanford Law Review* 49 (1997): 1065, 1070–74.

4. Campbell J. Gibson and Emily Lennon, "Historical Census Statistics on the Foreign-born Population of the United States: 1850–1990," U.S. Census Bureau, Population Division, February 1991, at www.census.gov/population/www/documentation/twps0029/twps0029.html. For data on Chicago, see Walter Nugent, "Demography: Chicago as a Modern World City," in *Encyclopedia of Chicago*, ed. James Grossman, Ann Durkin Keating, and Janice L. Reiff (2004), available online at www.encyclopedia.chicagohistory.org/. See also Rudolph J. Vecoli, "Italians," *Encyclopedia of Chicago* (2005). Italian immigration to Chicago began in the 1850s, and by 1880 there were 1,357 people from Italy in Chicago, most from the northern regions, especially the area around Liguria. For discussions of the problems of immigrants in the courts, see "He Realizes the Danger," *Chicago Times*, January 21, 1889, 1–2, a sermon criticizing the treatment of immigrants in the criminal justice system in Chicago; and "Address by Charles Evans Hughes to the 42d Annual Meeting of the New York State Bar Association, Jan. 17, 1919," quoted in David L. Bazelon, "The Morality of the Criminal Law," *Southern California Law Review* 49 (1975–1976): 385, 400.

5. Jeffrey Adler, *First in Violence, Deepest in Dirt: Homicide in Chicago, 1875–1920* (Cambridge: Harvard University Press, 2006), 169; Jeffrey Adler, "'It Is His First Offense. We Might as well Let Him Go': Homicide and Criminal Justice in Chicago, 1875–1920," *Journal of Social History* 40 (2006): 5, 6, 14–17.

6. For Borrono, see case entry, "Homicide in Chicago, 1870–1930, September 13, 1874." For Simoni, see case entry, "Homicide in Chicago, 1870–1930, April 29, 1878"; Rudolph John Vecoli, "Chicago's Italians prior to World War I: A Study of Their Social

and Economic Adjustment" (Ph.D. dissertation, University of Wisconsin, 1963), 65–66; "Simoni," *Chicago Tribune*, September 17, 1878, 8; "Simoni," *Chicago Tribune*, October 2, 1878, 8. For Sturla, see "The Girl's Career in Baltimore," *Chicago Tribune*, July 11, 1882, 3; "The Stiles Murder," *Chicago Tribune*, July 12, 1882, 8; "The Courts," *Chicago Tribune*, November 21, 1882, 6. Sturla was treated like others who killed abusive lovers, adulterous spouses, or their paramours; see Adler, "His First Offense," 11–12; Adler, *First in Violence*, 99–119.

7. Laura F. Edwards, *The People and Their Peace: Legal Culture and the Transformation of Inequality in the Post-revolutionary South* (Chapel Hill: University of North Carolina, 2009); Michael J. Pfeifer, *Rough Justice: Lynching and American Society, 1874–1947* (Urbana: University of Illinois Press, 2004); W. Fitzhugh Brundage, *Lynching in the New South: Georgia and Virginia, 1880–1930* (Urbana: University of Illinois Press, 1993); Christopher Waldrep, *Roots of Disorder: Race and Criminal Justice in the American South* (Urbana: University of Illinois Press, 1998).

8. Elizabeth Dale, *The Rule of Justice: The People of Chicago versus Zephyr Davis* (Columbus: Ohio State University Press, 2001).

1—An Italian Murder

1. Until further notice, unless otherwise noted all the articles cited in this note and those that follow were published May 2, 1885. "Another Trunk Mystery," *Chicago Tribune*, 5 (quote, describing trunk and also supplying details about the label and train route); "Mystery of a Trunk," *Chicago Herald*, 1; "Dead in a Trunk," *Pittsburg Dispatch*, 1; "A Mysterious Corpse at Pittsburg," *Washington Post*, 1; "Found in a Trunk," *Chicago Times*, 8; "Three Men Hanged," *New York Times*, November 15, 1885, 7; "The Pittsburg Mystery," *Chicago Tribune*, May 6, 1885, 1.

2. "Mystery of a Trunk," *Chicago Herald*, 1; "Dead in a Trunk," *Pittsburg Dispatch*, 1; "Another Trunk Mystery," *Chicago Tribune*, 5; "The Trunk Murders," *Atlanta Constitution*, May 4, 1885, 4. But see "Found in a Trunk," *Chicago Times*, 8 (station master's name was Jennings).

3. "Dead in a Trunk," *Pittsburg Dispatch*, 1 (flecked with blood and "other matter," mention of receipt); "Found in a Trunk," *Chicago Times*, 8 (quote; blood flecked face, mentions receipt); "Placed It in a Trunk," *Chicago Times*, 8 (blood and vomit on victim's face); "A Mysterious Corpse at Pittsburg," *Washington Post*, 1 (advanced stage of decomposition, face badly discolored and bloated); "Mystery of a Trunk," *Chicago Herald*, 1 (partly decomposed, smooth-shaven face, money order in pocket); "Another Trunk Mystery," *Chicago Tribune*, 5 (money order and details); "Placed It in the Trunk Alive," *Chicago Times*, May 3, 1885, 15 (money order and details); "Who Killed Caruso?" *Chicago Herald*, May 3, 1885, 1 (money order); "Domestic," *Chicago Daily Inter Ocean*, 1 (money order).

4. "Inquest Held," *Pittsburg Dispatch*, 1; "A Mysterious Corpse at Pittsburg," *Washington Post*, 1.

5. "Inquest Held," *Pittsburg Dispatch*, 1 (quote); "Mystery of a Trunk," *Chicago Herald*, 1 (coroner concluded the body had undoubtedly been dead several days); "Another Trunk Mystery," *Chicago Tribune*, 5; "Found in a Trunk," *Chicago Times*, 8.

6. Until further notice all newspapers are dated May 3, unless otherwise noted. "The Pittsburg Trunk Mystery," *Washington Post*, 1 (reporting that Mrs. Bonistalli, of Pittsburg, identified the corpse as that of her brother, and another man, Antonio Sabino, confirmed the identification); "The Pittsburgh Mystery," *Chicago Tribune*, 10 (Mrs. Bonistalli and

Antonio Sablino both identify the body as Pietro Caruso, Bonistalli's brother); "The Trunk Mystery," *Milwaukee Daily Sentinel*, 6 (same); "A Ghastly Mystery," *Atlanta Constitution*, 3 (noting that an Italian woman had identified the body as that of her brother, and that identification was confirmed by one of Caruso's "former associates"). But see "Gazed at by Hundreds," *Chicago Times*, 15 (three people all believe they know the dead man, though they all believe he is a different person); "Who Killed Caruso?" *Chicago Herald*, 1 (onlookers identify corpse as different people); "The Tragedy at Home," *Pittsburg Dispatch*, May 2, 1885, 1 (police decide none of the identifications are adequate).

7. "Another Trunk Mystery," *St. Louis Globe-Democrat*, May 2, 1885, 2; "Gazed at by Hundreds," *Chicago Times*, May 3, 1885, 15 (Coyle specifically recalled that the man had the "features" of an Irishman).

8. "Another Trunk Mystery," *Chicago Tribune*, May 2, 1885, 5 (no one at the Chicago baggage office could remember the man or men who brought the trunk in); "The Pittsburgh Mystery," *Chicago Tribune*, May 3, 1885, 10 (J. O'Brien recalled two Italians checked the trunk in around 11 in the morning); "Mystery of a Trunk," *Chicago Herald*, May 2, 1885, 1 (three Italians); "Another Trunk Mystery," *St. Louis Globe-Democrat*, May 2, 1885, 2 (same); "The Tragedy at Home," *Pittsburg Dispatch*, May 3, 1885, 1 (same); "The Caruso Murder," *Chicago Tribune*, May 7, 1885, 3 (three Italians).

9. "The Pittsburgh Mystery," *Chicago Tribune*, May 3, 1885, 10; "Who Killed Caruso?" *Chicago Herald*, May 3, 1885, 1; "Placed It in the Trunk Alive," *Chicago Times*, May 3, 1885, 15; "The Stranglers," *Pittsburg Dispatch*, May 2, 1885, 1 (Joseph Fillio). Entry for "Poli, Joseph, confectioner," *The Lakeside Annual Business Directory of the City of Chicago, 1885* (Chicago: Donnelly, Gassette & Lloyd, 1885), 1109.

10. "Placed It in the Trunk Alive," *Chicago Times*, May 3, 1885, 15 (Russo "generally answers the description of the man who brought the ticket to Pittsburg and shipped the trunk which contained the dead man"; the paper added that Russo's wagon also appeared to be the vehicle that transported the trunk to the station); "Who Killed Caruso?" *Chicago Herald*, May 3, 1885, 1 (baggage men not able to identify Russo or the others); "Another Trunk Mystery," *Chicago Tribune*, May 2, 1885, 5 (reporting that no one at the Chicago baggage office could remember the man or men who brought the trunk in); "Placed It in the Trunk Alive," *Chicago Times*, May 3, 1885, 15 (Russo first claimed he did not know anyone named Caruso, then admitted he had known Caruso in Sicily, but not in Chicago); "The Pittsburgh Mystery," *Chicago Tribune*, May 3, 1885, 10 (reporting that Russo vaguely recalled buying a money order for an unknown Italian in late February); "Pittsburgh's Trunk Mystery," *New York Times*, May 3, 1885, 2 (Russo recalled buying a money order for Caruso and gave him the receipt for it on March 1); "Who Killed Caruso?" *Chicago Herald*, May 3, 1885, 1 (same).

11. "The Pittsburgh Mystery," *Chicago Tribune*, May 3, 1885, 10 (Russo an Italian "boss," a "money-lender with Shylock proclivities"); Luciano John Iorizzo, "Italian Immigrants and the Impact of the *Padrone* System" (Ph.D. dissertation, Syracuse University, 1966), 78–82 (padroni and children).

12. "Immigration," *Bangor Daily Whig & Courier*, August 22, 1873, 2 (police officer's testimony in a New York City trial); Charles Loring Brace, *The Dangerous Classes of New York and Twenty Years among Them* (New York, 1872), 194–96 (international problem of padroni as manifest in New York); "Honor to the Italians," *Daily Arkansas Gazette*, October 8, 1873, n.p. (padrone run out of town in Little Rock); United States v. Ancarola (New York, 1880) (trial of suspected padrone in New York).

13. Iorizzo, "Italian Immigrants," 81–82 (various government activities with respect to child labor and padroni).

14. "The Padrone System," *Chicago Tribune*, January 16, 1885, 8 (the Chicago Italian consul declared there were very few Italian children enslaved to padroni in that city); "Swindling Poor Italians," *Chicago Daily News*, May 15, 1885, 1 (padroni enticing and exploiting adult immigrants); "Swindling Italian Laborers," *New York Times*, May 14, 1885, 5; Iorizzo, "Italian Immigrants," 58–92 (sketching the history of this shift); Alien Contract Labor Law or Foran Act, February 26, 1885, c. 164, 23 Stat. 332, 8 USC.

15. Humbert S. Nelli, ed., "The *Padrone* System: An Exchange of Letters," *Labor History* 17 (1976): 406; John Koren, "The *Padrone* System and the *Padrone* Bank," *Bulletin of the Department of Labor* 9 (1897): 113, 135–39; Humbert S. Nelli, *Italians in Chicago, 1880–1930: A Study in Ethnic Mobility* (New York: Oxford University Press, 1970), 56–59; Gunther Peck, "Reinventing Free Labor: Immigrant Padrones and Contract Laborers in North America, 1885–1925," *Journal of American History* 83 (1996): 848, 850–51 and n8; Jared N. Day, "Credit, Capital, and Community: Informal Banking in Immigrant Communities in the United States, 1880–1924," *Financial History Review* (2002): 65, 72.

16. Nelli, "Italian *Padrone* System" (padroni acted as employment agencies and were not uniformly bad for workers); Peck, "Reinventing Free Labor" (exploitation in the padrone's relation to workers); "The Pittsburgh Mystery," *Chicago Tribune*, May 3, 1885, 10 (description of Russo); "The Trunk Mystery," *Chicago Tribune*, May 4, 1885, 5 (witness changes story, claims "the murderer" nickname belonged to another Russo).

17. "The Pittsburg Mystery," *Chicago Tribune*, May 3, 1885, 10; "Who Killed Caruso?" *Chicago Herald*, May 3, 1885, 1; "Murdered for His Money," *Chicago Herald*, May 4, 1885, 1; "The Trunk Mystery," *Chicago Tribune*, May 4, 1885, 5 (Caruso's companion was Lawrence Rider). See entry for "Ryder, Lorenz, grocer," in *Lakeside Directory, 1885*, 1197. According to the 1880 census, Ryder lived over his candy shop on Rebecca Street. "Ryder, Lorenz," U.S. Census Bureau, *Tenth Annual Census, 1880: Chicago, Cook County, Illinois*, roll 190, page 242, line 19 (Ryder a grocer and immigrant from Wurtenberg).

18. "The Trunk Mystery," *Chicago Tribune*, May 4, 1885, 5; "Murdered for His Money," *Chicago Herald*, May 4, 1885, 1.

19. "Important Decision by Judge Moran as to What Constitutes a Peddler," *Chicago Tribune*, August 4, 1882, 7 (distinguishing between salesmen and peddlers); "Rotten Fruit," *Chicago Tribune*, September 4, 1881, 6 (Joseph Walker ran a fruit store at North Clark Street that supplied fruit stands around the city); "Rotten Fruit," *Chicago Tribune*, September 17, 1881, 8 (owner of fruit store is "the chief of a brigade of Italian and other street vendors, some thirty in number, whom he starts out every afternoon at about 5 o'clock with little go-carts to peddle out the stuff which he packs himself").

20. See, for example, A.R.D., "Letter to the Editor," *Chicago Tribune*, June 19, 1881, 16; "The Retail Grocers," *Chicago Tribune*, September 21, 1881, 8 (retail grocers object to peddlers and call for stricter licensing); "Rotten Fruit," *Chicago Tribune*, September 4, 1881, 6 (peddler charged with selling rotten fruit claimed he got it from the store he bought fruit at); "Rotten Fruit," *Chicago Tribune*, September 17, 1881, 8 (Turner owns store that was charged with supplying peddlers with rotten fruit); "Thieving Peddlers," *Chicago Tribune*, June 4, 1881, 3 (advising office workers to be on the lookout for thieves pretending to be peddlers but actually stealing items from offices); "Les Enfants Perdus," *Chicago Tribune*, August 6, 1881, 14 (complaints about their thieving and general immorality).

21. William J. Novak, *The People's Welfare: Law and Regulation in Nineteenth-Century America* (Chapel Hill: University of North Carolina Press, 1996), 87, 94–102 (regulation of peddlers). "Citizens' Association," *Chicago Tribune*, October 22, 1880, 12 (association's annual report); *Daily Inter Ocean*, August 25, 1881, 1 (police crackdown on peddlers' bad goods); "The City-Hall," *Chicago Tribune*, January 4, 1880, 8 (licensing); "A New License

Ordinance," *Chicago Tribune*, March 5, 1882, 8 (licensing); "Peddlers' Licenses," *Chicago Tribune*, April 16, 1882, 7 (fee of $10, reduced to $5); *Chicago Tribune*, February 27, 1883, 4 (bill raised the cost of all licenses); "A Street Peddler's Refuge," *Chicago Tribune*, January 24, 1885, 7 (federal land).

22. See, for example, "Some Nuisances," *Chicago Tribune*, June 1, 1873, 11 (noisy elements); "Being Polite to Peddlers," *Chicago Tribune*, August 21, 1876, 8 (constant interruptions by peddlers); "Obstructing the Sidewalk," *Chicago Tribune*, December 23, 1876, 7 (peddlers blocked sidewalks at State and Madison); "Down with Peddlers," *Chicago Tribune*, September 9, 1877, 16 (the noise peddlers made in residential neighborhoods).

23. "Found in a Trunk," *Chicago Times*, May 2, 1885, 8 (well dressed); "On the Trail," *Pittsburg Dispatch*, May 2, 1885, 2 (well dressed, silk underclothes); "Another Trunk Mystery," *Chicago Tribune*, May 2, 1885, 5 (silk underclothes, Congressional gaiters); "Another Trunk Murder," *St. Louis Globe-Democrat*, May 2, 1885, 2 (well-dressed, grey plaid pants, silk underwear); but see also "Dead in a Trunk," *Pittsburg Dispatch*, May 2, 1885, 1 (poorly dressed). Advertisement for the Fair, *Chicago Tribune*, March 29, 1885, 1 (front page ad, Congressional gaiters on sale at $2.50); "Placed It in the Trunk Alive," *Chicago Times*, May 3, 1885, 15 (flashed his money); "Caruso's Brother," *Pittsburg Dispatch*, May 4, 1885, 1 (known to carry large sums of money); "The Caruso Murder," *Chicago Tribune*, May 7, 1885, 3 (large roll of money, which he liked to toss in the air in front of others); "Mystery Solved," *Pittsburg Dispatch*, May 8, 1885, 2 (carried large sums); "Who Killed Caruso?" *Chicago Herald*, May 3, 1885, 1 (frugal); "Murdered for His Money," *Chicago Herald*, May 4, 1885, 1 (frugal and quiet).

24. "Tracing Caruso's Murderers," *Chicago Times*, May 7, 1885, 3 (trip to Pittsburg). For the stalled investigation, see "The Trunk Mystery," *Chicago Tribune*, May 5, 1885, 8 (baffle inquiry); "The Trunk Mystery," *Chicago Tribune*, May 5, 1885, 8 (dago case). See also John J. Flinn and John Elbert Wilkie, *A History of the Chicago Police* (Chicago: Police Book Fund, 1887; reprint, New York: AMS Press, 1973), 345 (James H. Bonfield was a police detective, previously a deputy jailer).

25. Citali Seton, "The Secret Societies of Southern Italy: The Camorra, Feudalism and Brigandage, the Mafia," *Lippincott's Magazine of Popular Literature and Science* 143 (1879): 579, 590–92 (discussion of the mafia); "The Psychology of Murder," *International Review* 3 (January 1876): 73, 88–90 (Sicilian "maffia"); "The Murderous Mafia," *Daily Inter Ocean*, October 24, 1888, 8 (no mafia in Chicago); "Has Chicago a Mafia?" *Chicago Tribune*, October 24, 1888, 1 (yes); "Letter to the Editor," *Chicago Tribune*, October 26, 1888, 9 (rejecting the *Tribune*'s conclusion).

26. John Dickie, *Cosa Nostra: A History of the Sicilian Mafia* (London: Hodder and Stoughton, 2004), 68–69 (1874 study); "The Murderous Mafia," *Daily Inter Ocean*, October 24, 1888, 8 (1876 report). For stories about vendettas, see, for example, "An Arab Vendetta," *San Francisco Daily Evening Bulletin*, July 28, 1874, 2; "The Gallows in Italy," *St. Louis Globe-Democrat*, July 7, 1876, 2; "The Corsican Vendetta," *San Francisco Daily Evening Bulletin*, November 12, 1878, 2; "The Vendetta," *Daily Evening Bulletin*, February 1, 1879, 1; "Home of the Vendetta," *Globe-Democrat*, December 26, 1880, 11; "An Italian Vendetta," *Denver Daily Rocky Mountain News*, October 16, 1887, 9.

27. Santi Romano, *L'ordinamento giuridico* (1918; reprint, Firenze: Sansoni, 1967), 44, 111, 123–24; "The Mafia Is a Myth," *Daily Inter Ocean*, November 13, 1890, 2 (Mattei); Leopoldo Franchetti, *Condizioni politiche e amministrative della Sicilia* (1876; reprint, Rome: Donizelli, 2000), 100; H. L. Wayland, "Social Science in the Laws of Moses: Wages and Pledges, Dignity of Labor, Crime, Humanity," *Journal of Social Science* 23 (1883): 167.

28. Wayland, "Social Science in the Laws of Moses"; Brundage, *Lynching in the New*

South; Pfeifer, *Rough Justice*. For the antebellum roots of rough justice, see Elizabeth Dale, "Popular Sovereignty: A Case Study from the Antebellum Era," in *Constitutional Mythologies: New Perspectives on Controlling the State*, ed. Alain Marciano (New York: Springer, forthcoming). For more materials on this subject, see Appendix B.

29. Richard Gambino, *Vendetta* (New York: Doubleday, 1977), 88 (quoting a song, that the lynching of the Italians in New Orleans was done for "justice and fair play"); "Honor to the Italians," *Daily Arkansas Gazette*, October 8, 1873, 4 (mob runs padrone out of town); Adler, *First in Violence*, 35, 38–39 (tracing violence in Chicago to claims of honor and revenge).

2—Police Investigations

1. "Caruso Identified," *Chicago Times*, May 8, 1885, 3; "A Woman Is the Cause," *Chicago Herald*, May 8, 1885, 1 (identification of body); "To Return to Chicago," *Chicago Times*, May 8, 1885, 3 (arrest in New York); "The Trunk Is Here," *Chicago Herald*, May 6, 1885, 1. It is not clear who the woman was who went to New York with Gelardi; it seems that Agostino Cammaratta's wife was called Domenica (Ciancola) Cammaratta.

2. "The Italian Murder," *Chicago Tribune*, May 11, 1885, 1; Vecoli, "Chicago's Italians," 86, 92.

3. "The Italian Murder," *Chicago Tribune*, May 11, 1885, 1; "A Woman Is the Cause," *Chicago Herald*, May 8, 1885, 1 (Bonfield's observations about Gelardi's cooperation).

4. "The Caruso Murder," *Chicago Tribune*, May 7, 1885, 3 (unable to identify any of the men in custody); "A Woman Is the Cause," *Chicago Herald*, May 8, 1885, 1; entry for "Semple, Edward, trunks," in *Lakeside Directory, 1885*, at 1247.

5. "A Woman Is the Cause," *Chicago Herald*, May 8, 1885, 1 (suspects lived at 94 Tilden); "The Italian Murder," *Chicago Tribune*, May 8, 1885, 3 (describing the building at 94 Tilden); entry for "Dolan, Patrick, driver," *Lakeside Directory, 1885*, 414.

6. "The Caruso Murder," *Chicago Tribune*, May 7, 1885, 3 (quote); see also ibid., "May Moving Day," May 1, 1885, 4; "Moving Day," April 18, 1894, 36; "Moving Day," April 30, 1872, 4; "The May Moving," April 28, 1889, 4.

7. "The Caruso Murder," *Chicago Tribune*, May 7, 1885, 3; "A Woman Is the Cause," *Chicago Herald*, May 8, 1885, 1.

8. "The Italian Murder," *Chicago Tribune*, May 8, 1885, 3; "A Woman Is the Cause," *Chicago Herald*, May 8, 1885, 1; "The Arrests in Chicago," *Chicago Daily News*, May 8, 1885, 1 (spelling her name "Corbin"); "Imitators of Maxwell," *New York Times*, May 2, 1885, 1; entry for "Corbett, John, laborer," *Lakeside Directory, 1885*, at 351.

9. "A Woman Is the Cause," *Chicago Herald*, May 8, 1885, 1; "The Noose Is Tightening," ibid., May 9, 1885, 1 (reporting that another man, Bonaconte Salvatore, was arrested with Mercurio); Appendix A.

10. "The Trunk Mystery," *Chicago Daily News*, May 7, 1885, 1 (Russo's attorneys advised Bonfield they intended to get a writ of habeas corpus for their client); "Jurado Will Probably Confess," *New York Times*, May 12, 1885, 1 (Russo being released); "A Woman Is the Cause," *Chicago Herald*, May 8, 1885, 1.

11. "No Nearer the Light," *Chicago Herald*, May 10, 1885, 9 (Gelardi's silence on the train); "A Jury Secured," *Pittsburg Dispatch*, June 27, 1885, 1 (none of the defendants understood what was happening at trial); "Who Killed Caruso?" *Chicago Herald*, May 3, 1885, 1 ("neither James H. Bonfield nor John A. MacDonald [another officer assigned to the case] are experts in the Italian language").

12. "No Nearer the Light," *Chicago Herald*, May 10, 1885, 9 (a steady pumping); "A Woman in It," *Chicago Times*, May 8, 1885, 3 (police will attempt to make Gelardi "squeal"); "Gelardi's Part in the Crime," *Chicago Herald*, May 12, 1885, 4; "The Mystery Solved," *Chicago Times*, May 13, 1885, 8; "Affidavit of Kate Kane filed in support of petition for pardon for Giovanni Azari" (Azari subjected to abusive interrogation techniques, threatened with execution, transported from station to station, and physical violence).

13. "Gelardi's Part in the Crime," *Chicago Herald*, May 12, 1885, 4; "The Mystery Solved," *Chicago Times*, May 13, 1885, 8.

14. "The Mystery Solved," *Chicago Times*, May 13, 1885, 8; "Some One Will Swing," *Chicago Herald*, May 13, 1885, 1; "Nearer to the Gallows," *Chicago Herald*, May 15, 1885, 2 (Bova came in just before the trunk was taken away).

15. "The Mystery Solved," *Chicago Times*, May 13, 1885, 8; "Some One Will Swing," *Chicago Herald*, May 13, 1885, 1 (Azari denied he was present during the crime and claimed he concealed what he was later told about the incident for fear of assassination).

16. Nelli, *Italians in Chicago*, ch. 2; Vecoli, "Chicago's Italians," 99, 107–9, 165, 181; Nelson Moe, *The View from Vesuvius: Italian Culture and the Southern Question* (Berkeley and Los Angeles: University of California Press, 2002).

17. See Appendix A.

18. Ibid.

19. Ibid.; "Three Deaths for One," *Chicago Herald*, November 15, 1885, 9 (Silvestri blond); Vecoli, "Chicago's Italians," 117 (status differences); Donna Gabaccia, *From Sicily to Elizabeth Street: Housing and Social Change among Italian Immigrants, 1800–1920* (Albany: SUNY Press, 1984).

20. "Choked to Death," *Chicago Tribune*, May 13, 1885, 1; "Gelardi's Part in the Case," *Chicago Herald*, May 12, 1885, 4.

21. On police corruption and misconduct at the turn of the century, see National Commission on Law Observance and Enforcement (hereafter the Wickersham Commission), *Report on Lawlessness in Law Enforcement* (Washington, D.C.: Government Printing Office, 1931). For a sampling of stories on Bonfield's conduct: "He Disgraces Chicago," *Chicago Herald*, August 28, 1882, 1; "Editorial," *Chicago Herald*, September 12, 1882, 2. For other materials on Bonfield, see Appendix C.

22. "Opposed to Bonfield," *Chicago Daily News*, October 19, 1885, 1 (streetcar strike); "What Was the Secret?" *Chicago Daily News*, October 6, 1885, 1 (deathbed). For other reports on Bonfield, see Appendix C.

23. James R. Green, *Death in the Haymarket: A Story of Chicago, the First Labor Movement, and the Bombing that Divided Gilded Age America* (New York: Pantheon Books, 2006), 122–24 (Bonfield and Haymarket); John Bonfield, "Police Patrol-Wagon," patent no. 379266, filing date December 29, 1886, issue date March 13, 1888; "Judge Tuley's Rebuke," *Chicago Times*, January 9, 1889, 4; "The Anarchist Investigation," *Chicago Daily News*, January 5, 1889, 1; "Scored by Tuley," *Chicago Daily News*, January 31, 1889, 1; "Editorial," *Chicago Tribune*, February 3, 1889, 4 (Tuley's ruling would interfere with effective policing); "Gambling in Chicago," *Chicago Times*, January 9, 1889, 1–2 (protection racket). See Appendix C for other articles.

24. "The Trunk Is Here," *Chicago Herald*, May 6, 1885, 1 ("Officers Morris and Arodo are working on the trunk mystery case, but up to last night had discovered nothing of importance"); Nelli, *Italians in Chicago*, 75 (Arado's tenure on the force); "Criminal," *Chicago Tribune*, November 13, 1877, 8 (pickpocket); "In General," *Chicago Tribune*, June 23, 1885, 8 (assault of fellow officer); "An Officer in Trouble," *Chicago Tribune*, July 7, 1887, 5 (assault during an arrest); "Bacon's Fatal Shot," *Chicago Tribune*, February 1, 1894, 8

(death); "Killed a Comrade," *Daily Inter Ocean*, February 1, 1898, 5 (death, with biographical information).

25. "Choked to Death," *Chicago Tribune*, May 13, 1885, 1; entry for "Ginochio, John, Departo & Ginochio, liquors," *Lakeside Directory, 1885*, 548; Vecoli, "Chicago's Italians," 67–68; "The Murdered Italian," *Chicago Tribune*, June 28, 1885, 3 (Ginochio claims, McDonald's account); entry for "Ostrella, Joseph, musician," *Lakeside Directory, 1885*, 1066; "Someone Will Swing," *Chicago Herald*, May 13, 1885, 1 (Ostrella the interpreter); "Murder Will Out," *Daily Inter Ocean*, May 13, 1885, 7 (Ostrella was Dago Jo); "The Murdered Italian," *Chicago Tribune*, June 28, 1885, 3 (Joseph Romano testified he assisted Morris by going to Tilden Avenue and interpreting for him); "The Secret Out at Last," *Chicago Daily News*, May 12, 1885, 1 (Morris).

26. "Trying to Pump Jurado," *Chicago Daily News*, May 11, 1885, 1; "Choked to Death," *Chicago Tribune*, May 13, 1885, 1 (none of the suspects "could speak a word of English"); "Necks in Danger," *Chicago Tribune*, June 25, 1885, 10; "A Jury Secured," *Pittsburg Dispatch*, June 27, 1885, 1 (none of the defendants understood the state's attorney's opening statement). H. H. Vaughn, "Studies in Italian Linguistics," *Italica* 13 (September 1936): 74, 78 (Sicilian differed from Italian); H. H. Vaughn, "The Implications of Dialect in Italy," *Italica* 3 (September 1928): 56 (linguistic influences on Sicilian).

27. Franchetti, *Condizioni politiche*, 46. I want to thank my colleagues Howard Louthan and Andrea Sterk for helping me with the translation of this and other passages from Franchetti. For Ginochio's claim, see "Choked to Death," *Chicago Tribune*, May 13, 1885, 1.

28. Franchetti, *Condizioni politiche*, 46.

3—Brought before the Law

1. "The Italian Assassins," *Chicago Daily News*, May 13, 1885, 1; "The Italian Murderers," *Chicago Daily News*, May 23, 1885, 1. At trial Donahoe represented only Mercurio, while Bova was represented by Nathaniel Sears. "Five Italian Assassins," *Chicago Daily News*, June 23, 1885, 1.

2. Francis Wharton, *A Treatise on Criminal Pleading and Practice*, 8th ed. (Philadelphia: Kay and Brother, 1880), 49–50.

3. "Criminal," *Chicago Tribune*, November 18, 1875, 8 (Foote as police court justice); "The Justices," *Chicago Tribune*, April 17, 1879, 2 (opposition within the Democratic Party, based on trumped-up charges by those who resent Foote's reforming zeal); "Editorial," *Chicago Tribune*, March 20, 1883, 4 (hostility toward Foote).

4. "Nearer the Gallows," *Chicago Herald*, May 15, 1885, 2 (first indictment); "The Italian Murderers," *Chicago Tribune*, May 21, 1885, 8 (error in indictment discovered by a clerk); "Affidavit by Kate Kane, filed in support of petition for pardon for Giovanni Azari" (Azari's guilty plea); "Indictment for murder, May 21, 1885," State of Illinois v. Ignazio Silvestri et al., term no. 1293, no 17521, Criminal Court of Cook County, Cook County archives, Richard J. Daley Center, Chicago, Illinois; "In General," *Chicago Tribune*, June 18, 1885, 8 (trial date moved up from June 29, not clear why).

5. David A. Joens, "John W. E. Thomas and the Election of the First African American to the Illinois General Assembly," *Journal of the Illinois Historical Society* 94 (2001): 200; "Mr. Hawes Declines," *Chicago Tribune*, April 5, 1876, 2 (no interest in being Chicago city attorney); "Obituary: Kirk Hawes," *New York Times*, September 10, 1904, 9.

6. "Special Bail," *Daily Inter Ocean*, August 26, 1879, 2 (city attorney); "Wooden Signs," *Daily Inter Ocean*, November 20, 1879, 8; "Jurist Dies Suddenly," *Milwaukee Daily*

Journal, June 8, 1898, 6. See also "Gelardi's Awful Deed," *Chicago Herald*, June 28, 1885, 5 ("Nelson served as Grinnell's assistant" during Trunk Murder trial); "A History of the Crime," *Pittsburg Dispatch*, July 1, 1885, 1 ("Longenecker assisted"); "The Seventh Day," *Chicago Times*, July 1, 1885, 6 ("Walker served as Grinnell's assistant").

7. Paul Avrich, *The Haymarket Tragedy* (Princeton, N.J.: Princeton University Press, 1984), 268; "Desperate Boodlers," *Chicago Tribune*, February 17, 1887, 1, 2 (McGarigle's complaint); "M'Garigle Gets Off Easy," *Chicago Tribune*, June 1, 1899, 4 (return, plea, and fine); Richard Schneirov, *Labor and Urban Politics: Class Conflict and the Origins of Modern Liberalism in Chicago, 1864–1897* (Urbana: University of Illinois Press, 1998), 222 (1886 trial).

8. Entry for "Daniel Donahoe," in *Bench and Bar of Chicago*, 589; "Romantic Story of Notre Dame," *Chicago Tribune*, June 23, 1899, 43 (Notre Dame's law school graduates); "Political Meetings Today," *Chicago Tribune*, November 2, 1898, 3 (Donahoe and Altgeld speak at Tenth Ward meeting).

9. "Sears and Foster," in *Bench and Bar of Chicago*, 239.

10. "Obituary: Kate Kane Rossi," *Chicago Tribune*, November 23, 1928, 22 (University of Michigan); "Debut of Miss Kate Kane as a Platform Speaker," *Milwaukee Daily Sentinel*, February 25, 1881, 3 (economic injustice).

11. "Kate Kane in War-paint," *Milwaukee Daily Journal*, January 4, 1883, 3 (Kane protests when judge refers to two women as sluts); "After Kate Kane," ibid., April 23, 1883, 3 (attorneys seek her arrest).

12. "Kate Kane Presented with a Purse by Her Friends," *Milwaukee Daily Sentinel*, May 20, 1883, 4; "Kate Kane on Deck," September 14, 1883, 4 (letter signed by one hundred women in Milwaukee); "Kate Kane Will Run for Judge," *Boston Daily Advertiser*, July 21, 1893, 5; "Kate Kane Still Talks," *Milwaukee Daily Journal*, December 21, 1895, 5 (against the degraded position of women); "Woman Seeks Police Headship," *Christian Science Monitor*, April 15, 1911, 5.

13. "Five Italian Assassins," *Chicago Daily News*, June 23, 1885, 1 (representing Gelardi and Silvestri); "The Italian Murderers," *Chicago Tribune*, May 26, 1885, 8 (city's Italians asked to contribute a dollar apiece to set up a fund for the defendants); "The Murderers of Filippo Caruso," *Pittsburg Dispatch*, June 24, 1885, 1 (Baumann hired by "wealthy Italians"). On Baumann's career, see entry for "I. C. Harris, compiler," in *Colored Men's Professional and Business Directory of Chicago, 1886*, 21 (advertisement for Baumann's firm, which chiefly did mechanics lien and civil work). For more on Baumann, see Appendix B.

14. "Five Italian Assassins," *Chicago Daily News*, June 23, 1885, 1.

15. *Illinois Revised Statutes*, ch. 28, §§21, 23 (twenty peremptory challenges per defendant and for the state). Illinois courts read this to mean that the state got twenty peremptory challenges for each defendant. Seymour Dwight Thompson, *A Treatise on the Laws of Trials in Actions Civil and Criminal* (1889), 1:38–39; Elizabeth Dale, "*People v. Coughlin* and Criticisms of the Criminal Jury in Late Nineteenth-Century Chicago," *Northern Illinois University Law Review* 28 (2008): 515 (Coughlin trial); Green, *Death in the Haymarket*, 212 (Haymarket trial); Dale, *Rule of Justice* (Davis case). Jury selection in the Sturla trial lasted four days, from November 20 through the end of the day on November 23, 1882. See the coverage in the *Chicago Tribune*, November 21–24, 1882.

16. "The Italian Assassins," *Chicago Daily News*, June 23, 1885, 1. The law on how jurors should be selected was ambiguous. The statute required twelve potential jurors be in the box at all times, but the Illinois Supreme Court seemed to interpret it to allow the lawyers to pass jurors in panels of four. *Illinois Revised Statutes*, ch. 78, §21, Sterling Brothers Co. v. Pearl, 80 Ill. 251, 253–54 (1875) (apparently applying that interpretation). "The

court adjourned [the first day] without even one juror having been secured, so good is the general disinclination to serve upon this trial and so general has been the formation and expression of opinion upon the case." "The Five Italians," *Chicago Times*, June 24, 1885, 5. Most of the jurors rejected the first two days of trial were excused for cause because they claimed to have formed strong opinions about the defendants' guilt, though a few were excused because they were sick or claimed to oppose the death penalty on religious grounds. "Necks in Danger," *Chicago Tribune*, June 25, 1885, 10.

17. "Two Murder Trials," *Chicago Tribune*, June 25, 1885, 8. See also "Not a Juror Chosen Yet," *Chicago Daily News*, June 24, 1885, 1; "The Murdered Italian," *Chicago Tribune*, June 27, 1885, 3; "The Trunk Murder," *Chicago Times*, June 27, 1885, 6; "The Italian Murder Trial," *Chicago Daily News*, June 26, 1885, 1; "Becoming Very Tiresome," *Chicago Daily News*, June 25, 1885, 1 (Kavanaugh). The rule in Illinois was that "a juror ought to stand indifferent between the prosecution and the accused." Gates v. Illinois, 14 Ill. 433, 434 (1853). But there was no rule that a prospective juror who knew one of the attorneys in the case should be excused for cause. "The Italian Murder," *Chicago Tribune*, June 24, 1885, 8 (Sears and Donahoe use voir dire to argue their cases to the jurors).

18. See, for example, "The Italian Murder," *Chicago Tribune*, June 24, 1885, 8 (understood not a word); "Two Murder Trials," *Chicago Tribune*, June 25, 1885, 8 (prisoners interested spectators, entirely in the dark); "Necks in Danger," *Chicago Times*, June 25, 1885, 10 (quote); "A Jury Secured," *Pittsburg Dispatch*, June 27, 1885, 1 (defendants knew no English); "The Italian Murder, *Chicago Tribune*, June 24, 1885, 8 (quote).

19. "The Italian Murder," *Chicago Tribune*, June 24, 1885, 8 (twenty Italians visited the jail the day before the trial and attended the first morning of the trial); "Stranglers on Trial," *Chicago Herald*, June 24, 1885, 2 (Italians at trial, one woman spoke to Silvestri before the proceedings began); "Two Murder Trials," *Chicago Tribune*, June 25, 1885, 8 (Italians at the trial, especially Italian women); "A History of Crime," *Pittsburg Dispatch*, July 1, 1885, 1 (crowd of Italians at the trial). "The Murdered Italian," *Chicago Tribune*, June 27, 1885, 3 (jurors listed, some names misspelled). The information about the jurors' occupations comes from *The Lakeside Directory, 1885*, and the Manuscript Census, Cook County, Chicago, Illinois, 1880. The makeup of this jury was consistent with the juries in Chicago's criminal courts at the turn of the century. See Adler, "His First Offense," 15 (far more office workers or salesmen on juries than laborers).

20. "A Jury Secured," *Pittsburg Dispatch*, June 27, 1885, 1.

21. Ibid.

22. "Indictment for murder," May 21, 1885, State of Illinois v. Ignazio Silvestri et al., term no. 1293, no 17521, Criminal Court of Cook County, Cook County Archives, Richard J. Daley Center, Chicago, Illinois. "A Jury Secured," *Pittsburg Dispatch*, June 27, 1885, 1 (omits some details of his statement); "The Murdered Italian," *Chicago Tribune*, June 27, 1885, 3 (quotes). See also "The Trunk Murder," *Chicago Times*, June 27, 1885, 1 (Mercurio and Silvestri strangled Caruso). Until further notice, all newspaper dates are June 27 unless otherwise noted.

23. "The Trunk Murder," *Chicago Times*, 6 (defense opening statements); "Stranglers on Trial," *Chicago Herald*, 4 (Donahoe); "The Murdered Italian," *Chicago Tribune*, June 27, 1885, 3 (Sears).

24. "Stranglers on Trial," *Chicago Herald*, 4 (McMurray); "Bad for the Stranglers," *Chicago Daily News*, 1 (Semple); "The Trunk Murder," *Chicago Times*, 5; entry for Semple's store at 290 W. Madison, *Lakeside Directory, 1885*, 1247.

25. "Stranglers on Trial," *Chicago Herald*, 4 (Semple's problems with identification); "The Murdered Italian," *Chicago Tribune*, 3; "The Trunk Murder," *Chicago Times*, 6 ("rope,"

otherwise they spoke "gibberish"). But see "The Italian Murder," *Chicago Tribune*, May 15, 1885, 5 (Buckley identified Silvestri as one of the men who bought the rope, and Gelardi probably with him); entry for "Buckley, John, hardware," *Lakeside Directory, 1885*, 260.

26. "The Murdered Italian," *Chicago Tribune*, 3 (they moved out that morning); "Stranglers on Trial," *Chicago Herald*, 4 (quote); "Bad for the Stranglers," *Chicago Daily News*, 1 (he testified they all moved on April 30).

27. "The Murdered Italian," *Chicago Tribune*, 3 (Caruso and oranges, Mercurio stayed behind when the others moved out); "Stranglers on Trial," *Chicago Herald*, 4; "Bad for the Stranglers," *Chicago Daily News*, 1 (she saw some defendants carry a trunk upstairs, later saw others take it downstairs, Bova was out peddling "while the others moved the trunk"); "The Trunk Murder," *Chicago Times*, 6 (rain).

28. "The Murdered Italian," *Chicago Tribune*, 3 (Murphy saw Caruso around 6:30 a.m.); "The Trunk Murder," *Chicago Times*, 6 (Murphy saw Caruso at 8:30 a.m.); "Stranglers on Trial," *Chicago Herald*, 4 (Murphy and Clancy); entry for "Murphy, Michael, teamster, 77 Tilden Avenue," in *Lakeside Directory*, 1005; entry for "Clancy, Michael, horsetrainer," 92 Tilden Avenue, *Lakeside Directory*, 318.

29. "The Trunk Murder," *Chicago Times*, 6; "The Murdered Italian," *Chicago Tribune*, 3 (two other men with Gelardi); but see "Stranglers on Trial," *Chicago Herald*, 4 (Riordan sent to New York to make the identification; Gelardi showed him a ticket to Pittsburg).

30. "The Trunk Murder," *Chicago Times*, 6 (quote); "Stranglers on Trial," *Chicago Herald*, 4 (substance); "Bad Day for the Stranglers," *Chicago Daily News*, 1 (breakfast); "The Murdered Italian," *Chicago Tribune*, 3.

31. "Stranglers on Trial," *Chicago Herald*, 4 (Dressler); "Bad Day for the Stranglers," *Chicago Daily News*, 1; "The Trunk Murder," *Chicago Times*, 6; "The Murdered Italian," *Chicago Tribune*, 3; "Gelardi's Awful Deed," *Chicago Herald*, June 28, 1885, 5.

32. Until further notice, all newspapers are dated June 28 unless otherwise noted. "Gelardi's Awful Deed," *Chicago Herald*, 5 (interpreter); "Bad Day for the Stranglers," *Chicago Daily News*, June 27, 1885, 1 (broken English quote); "The Murdered Italian," *Chicago Tribune*, 3 (broken English). But see "For Their Lives," *Chicago Times*, 14 (trunk in courtroom was "precisely similar" to the trunk he carried).

33. "The Murdered Italian," *Chicago Tribune*, 3 (strangled before he was put in the trunk); "For Their Lives," *Chicago Times*, 14 (dead less than two days); "Gelardi's Awful Deed," *Chicago Herald*, 5; "Bad for the Stranglers," *Chicago Daily News*, June 27, 1885, 1. But see "Mystery of a Trunk," *Chicago Herald*, May 2, 1885, 1 (Hamilton estimated the body had been dead several days, but not more than three).

34. "Bad for the Stranglers," *Chicago Daily News*, June 27, 1885, 1 (general summary of the witnesses' testimony); "Gelardi's Awful Deed," *Chicago Herald*, 5 (witness knows Caruso, Azari, and Silvestri); "The Murdered Italian," *Chicago Tribune*, 3 (Broughton's testimony); "Bad for the Stranglers," *Chicago Daily News*, June 27, 1885, 1 (Broughton).

35. "For Their Lives," *Chicago Times*, 14 (quote); "The Murdered Italian," *Chicago Tribune*, 3, 14 (Hawes ordered Ostrella to translate with Navageto to listen closely to his translation); "Bad for the Stranglers," *Chicago Daily News*, June 27, 1885, 1.

36. "The Murdered Italian," *Chicago Tribune*, 3 (Filippo already in Chicago); "Gelardi's Awful Deed," *Chicago Herald*, 5 (two brothers came to Chicago together); passenger list, *Indipendente*, March 9, 1885, microfilm serial M237, microfilm roll M237_483, list no. 255, line no. 41 (Francesco); passenger list, *Indipendente*, January 14, 1884, microfilm serial M237, microfilm roll M237_473, line no. 17 (Filippo); "The Murdered Italian," *Chicago Tribune*, 3 (defendants lived at 75 Tilden); "Bad for the Stranglers," *Chicago Daily News*, June 27, 1885, 1 (moved to 75 Tilden after the murder); "For Their Lives," *Chicago*

Times, 14 (the same).

37. "Bad for the Stranglers," *Chicago Daily News*, June 27, 1885, 1; "The Murdered Italian," *Chicago Tribune*, 3 ("Your brother has all the money"); "For Their Lives," *Chicago Times*, 14 (Caruso loaned Azari money); "Gelardi's Awful Deed," *Chicago Herald*, 5 ($145; sent $50 to the old country "a few days before his death"); "The Murdered Italian," *Chicago Tribune*, 3. But see "Their Last Hours Spent in Prayer," *Chicago Herald*, November 15, 1885, 8 (Pasquale Bova-Conti lived at 95 Tilden Avenue).

38. Joseph Frederic Privitera, *Basic Sicilian: A Brief Reference Grammar* (New York: Mellen Press, 1998); Adam Ledgeway, *A Comparative Syntax: The Dialects of Southern Italy: A Minimalist Approach* (Oxford: Blackwell, 2000).

39. "For Their Lives," *Chicago Times*, 14.

40. "The Murdered Italian," *Chicago Tribune*, 14; "For Their Lives," *Chicago Times*, 14.

41. "For Their Lives," *Chicago Times*, 14; "Gelardi's Awful Deed," *Chicago Herald*, 5.

42. "Gelardi's Awful Deed," *Chicago Herald*, 5 (Nicholas Morris). There is no listing for Nicholas Morris in Chicago in the 1880 Manuscript Census for Chicago; entry for "Morris, Nicholas, police officer, Desplaines Avenue station," in *Lakeside Directory, 1885*, 489 (police officer at Desplaines Avenue); entry for "Morris, Nicholas, saloonkeeper," *Lakeside Directory, 1889*, 1271; "The Caruso Murder," *Chicago Tribune*, June 30, 1885, 2 (John Morris, "the Italian member of the force"); entry for "Morris, John, police," in *Lakeside Directory, 1885*, 489; Flinn and Wilkie, *Chicago Police*, 474 (Morris, John).

43. "Scored by Tuley," *Chicago Daily News*, January 31, 1889, 1 (police department needed a continuance, to do more investigation, but the officer sent in to represent the department had nothing to do with the case); Andrews v. Illinois, 117 Ill. 195, 198–99 (1886), discussing that witnesses before the grand jury had to be listed and the list given to the defense.

44. Until further notice, all newspapers are dated June 30 unless otherwise noted. "The Caruso Murder," *Chicago Tribune*, 2; "Self Convicted," *Chicago Times*, 1.

45. "Self Convicted," *Chicago Times*, 1.

46. Ibid.; "Saving Their Necks," *Chicago Herald*, 4; entry for "Ostrella, Joseph, musician," *Lakeside Directory, 1885*, 1866.

47. "Saving Their Necks," *Chicago Herald*, 4 (ability to comprehend the defendants); "Self Convicted," *Chicago Times*, 1 (the state also offered into evidence the money order found in Caruso's pocket and the photo of Caruso, but Hawes refused to admit them).

4—Justice Is Served

1. "Saving Their Necks," *Chicago Herald*, June 30, 1885, 4; "The Italian Murderers," *Daily Inter Ocean*, June 30, 1885, 8. Until further notice, all newspapers are dated June 30 unless otherwise noted.

2. "Saving Their Necks," *Chicago Herald*, 4.

3. Ibid. (quote); "The Caruso Murder," *Chicago Tribune*, 2. But see "The Italian Murderers," *Daily Inter Ocean*, 8 (Mercurio told a story "somewhat similar" to Bova's).

4. "The Caruso Murder," *Chicago Tribune*, 2.

5. Rex v. Lee Kun, quoted in Sascha Auerbach, *Race, Law, and "The Chinese Puzzle" in Imperial Britain* (New York: Palgrave MacMillan, 2009), 94 (due process and proper translations); Christopher Munn, "The Transportation of Chinese Convicts from Hong Kong, 1844-1858," *Journal of the Canadian Historical Association* 8 (1997): 113, 116 (Hong Kong); Carolyn A. Conley, "Wars among the Savages: Homicide and Ethnicity in the Vic-

torian United Kingdom," *Journal of British Studies* 44 (2005): 775. The range of languages that witnesses spoke at trials in the United States is suggested by a handful of trial records. See *Trial of Francisco Salvador* (1866), 40 (Spanish); *Trial of John H. Surratt* (1867), 850 (French); *Trial of the Impeachment of Patrick H. Laverty* (1886), 267–68 (German), 298–99 (German), 917 (German); *Trial of Ancarola* (1880), 13 (Italian); *Trial of Sarah Jane Robinson* (1888), 94 (Swedish); *Trial of John J. Corcoran*, 46 (1881) (Chinese, with interpreter).

6. For examples of how different states dealt with the issue, see Livar v. Texas, 26 Tex. Ct. App 115, 119 (1888) (state statute requires court interpreter whenever there was a witness who did not speak English, but statute did not mean a defendant who did not speak English was entitled to a court-appointed interpreter); Gardner v. Illinois, 106 Ill. 76, 83–85 (1883) (in a capital case, a defendant who spoke no English and did not understand the American legal system should have been given appointed counsel and a competent interpreter at his preliminary hearing); Louisiana v. Arbuno, 105 La. 719 (1900) (defendant challenged the competence of interpreter on appeal, claiming inaccuracies in the translation, but court refused to sustain the objections on the ground that they had not been made at trial).

7. Grace Abbott, "The Treatment of Aliens in the Criminal Court," *Journal of the American Institute of Criminal Law and Criminology* 2 (1912): 554, 558, 560–61 (rape victim); Matilda Fletcher Wiseman, *The Trial and Imprisonment of George W. Felts* (1907), 6, 102 (Felts was tried in Rockford, Illinois, in 1907, the trial judge failed to provide him with a sign interpreter). See also *Gardner* 106 Ill. at 81 (judge asked a lawyer to interpret for defendant in a preliminary hearing on a murder trial, the lawyer demurred as he could not translate the technical legal issues into German, the judge told him to go ahead anyway). For a similar incident, see *Trial of Theodosius Botkin* (1891), 982 (impeachment of a judge, one charge against him was that he had allowed the sister of a witness to act as interpreter, over the objections of defense counsel).

8. Abbott, "Treatment of Aliens," 560. See also Joan Colin and Ruth Morris, *Interpreters and the Legal Process* (Winchester, U.K.: Waterside Press, 1996), 17 (interpreters have to be able to translate competently both from and into English); "The Caruso Murder," *Chicago Tribune*, June 30, 1885, 2 (interpreters inadequate).

9. "The Italian Murder," *Chicago Tribune*, July 1, 1885, 8 (he claimed he went to the apartment at 94 Tilden Avenue frequently to arrange to have Azari purchase fruit from him, or to have Azari repair his shoes); "Gelardi's Wife a Terror," *Chicago Daily News*, June 30, 1885, 1; "The Caruso Murder," *Chicago Tribune*, June 30, 1885, 2.

10. "The Seventh Day," *Chicago Times*, July 1, 1885, 6. The Bourbons ruled the Kingdom of Naples and Sicily until the mid-nineteenth century. Lucy Riall, "Garibaldi and the South," in *Italy in the Nineteenth Century, 1796–1900*, ed. John A. Davis (Oxford: Oxford University Press, 2000), 132.

11. "Gelardi's Wife a Terror," *Chicago Daily News*, June 30, 1885, 1; "The Seventh Day," *Chicago Times*, July 1, 1885, 6. Kane also put McDonald back on the stand to testify that the police did not find Caruso's missing watch or any money on Azari. Baumann tried to subpoena other character witnesses for his clients (see defense subpoenas dated June 25, 26, 27, 1885), but the subpoenas were all returned by the sheriff marked "not found."

12. The instructions—which are not numbered but are labeled to show whether they were offered by the prosecution or the defense—may be found, along with Hawes's handwritten emendations, deletions, and notations ("given," "refused") in People v. Ignazio Silvestri et al., court file no. 1294. The state's instructions are typed, the instructions for the defense are handwritten. The two instructions relating to circumstantial evidence were both apparently presented by Baumann. The first provided the relevant part "Any particular

fact constituting but a single link in the necessary chain of evidence must be as well proved beyond a reasonable doubt as must the collective proof or the entire chain of essential evidence be proved beyond a reasonable doubt." The second provided the part "The court instructs the jury that circumstantial evidence alone will not warrant a conviction unless each material fact necessary to constitute the guilt is proved beyond a reasonable doubt, and unless each material fact is consistent with the other material facts and with the facts to be proved, and unless all combined produce conviction in the minds of the jury beyond a reasonable doubt, and unless all combined are consistent with the guilt of the accused and inconsistent with any other reasonable theory." Both instructions are found in the court file People v. Ignazio Silvestri et al., no. 1294.

13. The instruction on the confessions that Hawes refused to give told the jurors to consider the circumstances under which the defendants confessed: "The court instructs the jury that as a matter of law they are to take into consideration the way and manner in which the confessions of Ignazio Silvestri and Augustino Gelardi were obtained by officers Bonfield, McDonald, and Nicholas Morris the latter of whom acted as interpreter for the former officers." This instruction may have been refused because it referred to only two of the defendants, but this could easily have been remedied by adding other names to the list. While Azari testified, outside the presence of the jury, that he had been threatened, Baumann and Kane both tried to raise the question of whether the confessions were made under duress. "Saving Their Necks," *Chicago Herald*, June 30, 1885, 4; "The Caruso Murder," *Chicago Tribune*, June 30, 1885, 2. For the rule that confessions could not be admitted if they were made in response to threats or promises, see *Gates*, 14 Ill. at 436–37. For the instruction directing the jurors to find Bova and Mercurio not guilty, see the Instruction as the Form of the Verdict. Logg v. Illinois, 92 Ill. 598, 603 (1879) (reversible error to take contested issue of fact from the jury by means of an instruction).

14. Lyons v. Illinois, 137 Ill. 602 (1891); Reynolds v. Illinois, 83 Ill. 479, 480 (1876).

15. "The Seventh Day," *Chicago Times*, July 1, 1885, 6 (assistant state attorney); "The Italian Trio," *Chicago Tribune*, July 2, 1885, 2. Kane made a similar point in a petition for clemency that she filed on Azari's behalf, "Affidavit of Kate Kane filed in support of petition for pardon for Giovanni Azari." See Gail Bederman, *Manliness and Civilization: A Cultural History of Gender and Race in the United States, 1880–1917* (Chicago: University of Chicago Press, 1995) (contemporary notions of masculinity); Nick Salvatore, *Eugene V. Debs: Citizen and Socialist* (Urbana: University of Illinois Press, 1982), 58–59 (nineteenth-century theories of manhood).

16. "Pleading for the Italians," *Chicago Daily News*, July 1, 1885, 1 ("men of no mental balance," "imbeciles or idiots"); "A Gallows for Three," *Chicago Herald*, July 2, 1885, 1 ("imbeciles" and "not legally responsible"); "Halters for Three," *Chicago Times*, July 2, 1885, 2; Cesare Lombroso, *L'uomo delinquente* (1876); Mary Gibson, *Born to Crime: Cesare Lombroso and the Origins of Biological Criminality* (Westport, Conn.: Praeger, 2002), 21–22.

17. "Extreme Penalty," *Daily Inter Ocean*, July 2, 1885, 8.

18. Verdict filed July 1, 1885, re defendants Gelardi, Silvestri, and Azari. Jurors in Illinois determined guilt and set the sentence; Blevings v. Illinois, 2 Ill. (1 Scam.) 171, 172 (1835); Verdict filed July 1, 1885, re defendants Bova and Mercurio; "The Italian Trio," *Chicago Tribune* July 2, 1885, 2.

19. "The Italian Trio," *Chicago Tribune*, July 2, 1885, 2 (Francesco Caruso threatens revenge on Bova and Mercurio); "Frightened to Death," *Chicago Herald*, July 3, 1885, 4 (Francesco Caruso is arrested at the close of trial, after being found with razor).

20. "Criminal Courts," *Chicago Tribune*, July 3, 1885, 8 (Baumann motion); "The

Italian Murderers," *Chicago Tribune*, July 4, 1885, 8 (Kane motion); "Criminal Courts," *Chicago Tribune*, August 1, 1885, 8 (Kane affidavit); "A Batch of Criminals," *Chicago Tribune*, August 2, 1885, 16 (transcript will cost $400); "Affidavit of Kate Kane in support of motion for a new trial," filed on behalf of defendant Azari, July 31, 1885; "Motion to Obtain Transcript," filed on behalf of defendant Azari, August 1, 1885 (Kane's efforts to prepare motion).

21. "Criminal Courts," *Chicago Tribune*, August 1, 1885, 8 (hearing on the motion for a new trial was scheduled for that morning); "A Batch of Criminals," *Chicago Tribune*, August 2, 1885, 16 (motion continued until September); "The Italian Murderers," *Chicago Tribune*, September 8, 1885, 8 (motion for a new trial hearing, scheduled for September 7, 1885, rescheduled at the request of Kane and Baumann); "The Italian Murderers," *Chicago Tribune*, September 20, 1885, 16; "The Italian Murderers," *Chicago Tribune*, September 20, 1885, 16. See also the spare "Motion for a New Trial," filed on behalf of Giovanni Azari, on September 7, 1885, in People v. Ignazio Silvestri et al.

22. "They Will Hang," *Chicago Tribune*, October 25, 1885, 6; Adler, "His First Offense," 11 (conviction rate in 1885). The defendants who were executed in the 1880s were James Tracy, convicted of killing a police officer in 1882; Azari, Gelardi, and Silvestri, convicted of killing Filippo Caruso in 1885; Frank Mulkowski, convicted of killing Agnes Kledziak in 1885; four of the Haymarket defendants (August Spies, Albert Parsons, George Engel, and Adolph Fischer) in 1887; and Zephyr Davis, convicted of killing Maggie Gaughan in 1888. Hawes was the trial judge for the Trunk Murder, Mulkowski, and Zephyr Davis. Chicago Police Department, *Homicides and Other Records, 1870–1910*, roll no. 30-2293, Illinois State Archives, Springfield, Illinois.

23. "They Will Hang," *Chicago Tribune*, October 25, 1885, 6; "The Italian Murderers," *Chicago Tribune*, October 24, 1885, 7.

24. "They Will Hang," *Chicago Tribune*, October 25, 1885, 6; Motion in Arrest, filed on behalf of Giovanni Azari, on October 24, 1885, in People v. Ignazio Silvestri et al.; "Application for pardon of Giovanni Azari," no. 611, filed November 12, 1885 (Azari could not afford to obtain the transcript or file the appeal).

25. "Two of the Italians Freed," *Chicago Herald*, July 1, 1885, 2 (incident in Sicily); "The Italians Weep," *Chicago Tribune*, July 3, 1885, 8; "The Italian Murderers," *Chicago Tribune*, July 4, 1885, 8; "In Paroxysms of Fright," *Chicago Daily News*, July 2, 1885, 1. See also "Grant's Death at Hand," *Chicago Tribune*, July 1, 1885, 1; "The Militia Called Out," *Chicago Tribune*, July 15, 1885, 1 (strike in Michigan); "Ready for Blood Today," *Chicago Tribune*, July 18, 1885, 3 (strikes in Ohio and southern Illinois); "The Strikers Firm," *Chicago Tribune*, July 21, 1885, 2 (Ohio); "Cheyennes Hemmed In," *Chicago Tribune*, July 18, 1885, 1; "A Fight to the Death," *Chicago Tribune*, July 20, 1885, 1; "Tramp, Tramp, Tramp," *Chicago Tribune*, July 1, 1885, 1; "The Street-Car Men's Strike," *Chicago Tribune*, July 1, 1885, 4; "Anarchists in Array," *Chicago Tribune*, July 27, 1885, 5. On the flood, see "And a Flood Came," *Chicago Tribune*, August 3, 1885, 1; Libby Hill, "The Chicago Epidemic of 1885: An Urban Legend?" *Journal of Illinois History* 9 (2006): 154; "Quiet at Pullman," *Chicago Daily News*, October 1, 1885, 1 (fear of a strike).

26. "A Cruel Death," *Chicago Tribune*, August 8, 1885, 8 (Fitzgerald murder). See also *Chicago Homicide and Other Records* (Ann Walsh, Ann Fitzgerald's other name, murdered on August 7, 1885); "Chicago Tragedies," *Chicago Tribune*, August 24, 1885, 2 (Fitzgerald and O'Leary); "Dead Wife," *Chicago Tribune*, August 23, 1885, 3 (Kledziak).

27. Marco Soresina, "Pietro Ellero and the Debate on the Death Penalty, 1861–1865," *Risorgimento* 38 (1986): 96 (nationwide effort beginning to end capital punishment); Franklin E. Zimring, *American Capital Punishment* (New York: Oxford University Press,

2004), 18 (Italy abolished the death penalty in 1889). Cf. "Three Dangling Corpses," *Chicago Daily News*, November 14, 1885, 1 (Azari tells reporters that the death penalty has been eliminated in Italy); "Eternity Drawing Nigh," *Chicago Daily News*, November 13, 1885, 1 (priests); "To Hang at High Noon," *Chicago Herald*, November 14, 1885, 1. On the two priests, see Nelli, *Italians in Chicago*, 189; Vecoli, "Chicago's Italians," 47–49. "The Italian Murderers," *Chicago Tribune*, July 4, 1885, 8, and "Affidavit of Kate Kane filed on behalf of the petition for clemency for Giovanni Azari" (bills).

28. See Petition of Kathryn Kane, "Application for the pardon of Giovanni Azari." As a matter of Illinois law, a petition for clemency (or a pardon, the two terms were effectively interchangeable) could seek either to have the judgment against the defendant set aside entirely or to reduce the sentence. Holliday v. Illinois, 10 Ill. 214, 216 (1848). John Corbett, 172 Madison, Chicago (no relation, apparently, to the Corbetts of Tilden Avenue), to Richard Oglesby, dated November 12, 1885; Christian Kohlsaat, First National Bank Building, Chicago, to Oglesby, dated November 12, 1885; unknown, Chicago, to Oglesby, dated November 13, 1885 (it is unclear which of the two white attorneys the letter writer considered insufficiently trained). All three letters are in "Application for a pardon for Giovanni Azari."

29. "To Die Tomorrow," *Chicago Herald*, November 13, 1885, 2. Oglesby's note is on the front of the pardon packet; the letter from Julius Grinnell to Richard J. Oglesby, dated November 10, 1885, is a separate sheet within the file; Hawes's note to the governor, dated November 11, 1885, is at the bottom of Kane's petition, under her signature. The power to pardon was granted by statute to the governor, Illinois ch. 104A, but pardons were politically delicate. When Illinois's Governor Altgeld pardoned some of the Haymarket defendants on the grounds that their convictions were not supported by the evidence, he was roundly denounced both locally and nationally. "Notes," *Albany Law Journal* 55 (1897): 21.

30. "Three at Once," *Chicago Time*, November 15, 1885, 13. The event was noticed outside of the city as well. "In and about Chicago," *Christian Union*, November 19, 1885, 6 (three Italians hanged for "cold blooded murder"); "Three Men Hanged," *New York Times*, November 15, 1885, 7.

31. "Three at Once," *Chicago Times*, November 15, 1885, 13.

32. "Their Dangling Corpses," *Chicago Daily News*, November 14, 1885, 1 (Azari's question); "Three at Once," *Chicago Times*, November 15, 1885, 13 (two thousand present); "To Hang at High Noon," *Chicago Herald*, November 14, 1885, 1 (ladies); "Caruso Avenged," *Chicago Tribune*, November 15, 1885, 3 (fifteen hundred present). But see "Three Men Hanged," *New York Times*, November 15, 1885, 7 (three hundred present).

33. Until further notice, all newspapers are dated November 15 unless otherwise noted. "Three at Once," *Chicago Times*, 13 (no translator, prayers); "Three Dangling Corpses," *Chicago Daily News*, November 14, 1885, 1 (one of the priests interpreted). On the defendants' reactions on the gallows platform: "Three Deaths for One," *Chicago Herald*, 8 (different reactions); "Caruso Avenged," *Chicago Tribune*, 3 (all defendants moved by prayers).

34. "Three Men Hanged," *New York Times*, 7 (Azari died slowly); "Three at Once," *Chicago Times*, 13 (Azari died slowly, by strangling); "Three Dangling Corpses," *Chicago Daily News*, November 14, 1885, 1 (poetic justice). But see "Three Deaths for One," *Chicago Herald*, 8 (one doctor concluded that Azari died first); "Caruso Avenged," *Chicago Tribune*, 3 (hanging went without a hitch).

35. Advertisement for the Dime Museum, *Chicago Tribune*, 15; Pfeifer, *Rough Justice*, 48 (ritual display of items relating to a lynching, including body parts); "The Chamber of Horrors," *Chicago Tribune*, November 16, 1885, 8 (Italians).

5—The Triumph of Common Sense

1. "To Die To-morrow," *Chicago Herald*, November 13, 1885, 2; "Editorial," *Chicago Times*, November 14, 1885, 4; Stuart Banner, *The Death Penalty: An American History* (Cambridge: Harvard University Press, 2002), 144–68.

2. "They Will Hang," *Chicago Tribune*, October 25, 1885, 6.

3. "For Their Lives," *Chicago Times*, June 28, 1885, 14 (Filippo arrived eighteen months before his murder); "Frightened to Death," *Chicago Herald*, July 3, 1885, 4 (Filippo's bank). This estimate of the income for fruit peddlers in Chicago in 1885 is based on data from the 1890s. In the middle of that decade, when the wages for Sicilians working in sugar fields in Louisiana dropped to 50–60 cents a day, many moved to Chicago to take work as unskilled labor there. Vecoli, "Chicago's Italians," 109. This sets a low-end wage of about $3.50 a week, around $175.00 a year, suggesting that unskilled laborers in Chicago, including fruit peddlers, made more than that. The conclusion is confirmed by a Bureau of Labor Statistics study prepared in the mid-1890s, which found that the average weekly income of fruit peddlers in Chicago was $4.33 a week (roughly $237 a year), assuming the peddler worked fifty weeks a year. Table X, Commissioner of Labor, *The Italians in Chicago: A Social and Economic Study* (Washington, D.C., 1897), 367–77; Cynthia Eastwood, "A Study of the Regulations of Chicago Street Vendors" (Ph.D. diss., University of Illinois, Chicago, 1988), 47–48. But a closer look at the data on specific workers reveals that, while some earned this much and did work fifty or even fifty-two weeks per year, others worked far less or earned far less. See, for example, Eastwood, "Chicago Street Vendors," at 127 (peddler worked thirty-three weeks as peddler, also held second job), 139 (two peddlers work fifty-two weeks a year, yearly earnings for each was less than $100, one worked forty-eight weeks as a peddler, held a second job, and earned just over $100), 127 (peddler worked thirty-three weeks as peddler), 141 (lame vegetable peddler worked fifty-two weeks, earned $156 for year), 143 (man worked as peddler forty-nine weeks, earned $115 for year, also worked three weeks as sewer digger; man worked forty-eight weeks as fruit peddler, earned $73 for year, also worked as a laborer for four weeks).

4. Jessica Snyder Sachs, *Corpse: Nature, Forensics, and the Struggle to Pinpoint Time of Death* (New York: Basic Books, 2002), 18–19; Vincent J. M. DiMaio and Suzanna E. Dana, *Handbook of Forensic Pathology* (Austin: Landes Bioscience, 1998), 22–23; "Dead in a Trunk," *Pittsburg Dispatch*, May 2, 1885, 1 (trunk opened "shortly after 5 o'clock"); Alfred Swaine Taylor, *A Manual of Medical Jurisprudence*, 11th ed. (Philadelphia: Lea Brothers & Co., 1892), 68–69.

5. "River and Weather," *Pittsburg Daily Post*, May 2, 1885, 4.

6. "An Inquest Held," *Pittsburg Dispatch*, May 2, 1885, 1 (describing the body); Taylor, *Medical Jurisprudence*, 416–17. "Rarely, one will have a manual strangulation in which there is neither external or internal evidence of trauma. This occurs when the victim was unconscious at the time they were assaulted and the amount of pressure to the neck was so minimal as not to produce either external or internal injury." DiMaio and Dana, *Forensic Pathology*, 144. See also "Dead in a Trunk," *Pittsburg Dispatch*, May 2, 1885, 1 (men in baggage car complained about the trunk's strong smell); "The Pittsburg Mystery," *Chicago Tribune*, May 3, 1885, 10 (body bloated, almost black); Sachs, *Corpse*, 21; DiMaio and Dana, *Forensic Pathology*, 24–25. Taylor also suggested that bodies killed suddenly might go into rigor more quickly and putrefy more rapidly, see *Medical Jurisprudence*, 68–69, which could have sped the process up more in this case than the climatic conditions would otherwise suggest.

7. C. T. McCormick, *Handbook of the Law of Evidence* (St. Paul: West Publishing, 1972), 316, quoted in Saul M. Kassim, "The Psychology of Confessions," *Annual Review of Law and Social Science* 4 (2008): 193, 194.

8. Paul V. Ford, "The Crime that Baffled Lincoln!" *Chicago Tribune*, January 28, 1951, C3 (Lincoln was one of the attorneys for the defendants); "Confessions as Evidence of Guilt," *Albany Law Journal* 11 (1875): 7; Wickersham Commission, *Report on Lawlessness*, 21. See also "Current Topics," *Albany Law Journal* 10 (1874): 98.

9. Hugo Adam Bedau and Michael L. Radelet, "Miscarriages of Justice in Potentially Capital Cases," *Stanford Law Review* 40 (1987): 21, 57, and table 6 (eleven of the cases they identified came from Illinois). See also Steven A. Drizin and Marissa J. Reich, "Heeding the Lessons of History: The Need for Mandatory Recording of Police Interrogation to Accurately Assess the Reliability and Voluntariness of Confessions," *Drake Law Review* 52 (2004): 619; Kassim, "Psychology of Confessions," 193, 194.

10. Kassim, "Psychology of Confessions," 193, 201.

11. Ibid., 201 (citing a number of studies).

12. Ibid., 201–2.

13. "Current Topics," *Albany Law Journal* 10 (1874): 98. For recent studies that confirm that article's intuition, see Kassim, "Psychology of Confessions," 195; Drizin and Reich, "Heeding the Lessons of History," 619; "Frightened to Death," *Chicago Herald*, July 3, 1885, 4 (defendants told they would be imprisoned).

14. Josiah William Smith, *A Manual of Common Law*, 1st American ed. (1871), 539.

15. Robert Ferrari, "The Immigrant in the New York County Criminal Courts," *Journal of the American Institute of Criminal Law and Criminology* 3 (1912): 194, 202. See also Louise de Koven Bowen, *The Colored People of Chicago* (Chicago: Juvenile Prevention Association, 1913), n.p. (describing a case where attorneys pressured a young black man, George W., to confess because they incorrectly believed he was guilty of the crime); Tom Wells and Richard A. Leo, *The Wrong Guys: Murder, False Confessions, and the Norfolk Four* (New York: New Press, 2009).

16. "Confessions as Evidence of Guilt," 7.

17. "They Will Hang," *Chicago Tribune*, October 25, 1885, 6.

18. On arrests, see Robert H. Vickers, *The Powers and Duties of Police Officers and Coroners* (Chicago, 1889), 12–13, 28, 55–58; on extradition, see Kentucky v. Dennison, 65 U.S. 66, 109 (1860). See also "Extradition of Fugitives from Justice," *Albany Law Journal* 10 (1874): 129.

19. Illinois Constitution of 1818, art. 8, sec. 9; see also *Illinois Revised Statutes*, ch. 38 §482 (right to counsel and to have counsel appointed); *Gardner*, 106 Ill. 76; Johnson v. Whiteside County, 110 Ill. 22, 24 (1884). Several years after the Trunk Murder case, the Illinois Supreme Court limited the right to some extent; see Fielden v. Illinois, 128 Ill. 595 (1890) (right to counsel limited to "trials at nisi prius only," not to post-conviction remedies), but this limited the right to representation *after* trial and would have had no impact on the defendants' rights in the Trunk Murder case.

20. Johnson v. Illinois, 22 Ill. 314, 318 (1959), citing United States v. Marchant et al., 23 U.S. 480, 482–83 (1827), holding that the rights of codefendants tried together were protected so long as each had an individual right to challenge jurors, which was the case in the Trunk Murder trial. Note that Illinois law modified English common law to the extent that it allowed accessories to be tried with principals and to testify at trial. Collins v. Illinois, 98 Ill. 584 (1881); White v. Illinois, 81 Ill. 333, 339 (1876) (where a codefendant's evidence is very damaging to defendant, a separate trial should be granted); and Gillespie v. Illinois, 176 Ill. 238, 242–43 (1898).

21. Illinois v. Dacey, 116 Ill. 555, 566-69 (1884); "Five Italian Assassins," *Chicago Daily News*, June 23, 1884, 1; "The Murderers of Filippo Caruso," *Pittsburg Dispatch*, June 24, 1885, 1. See also "Application for a pardon, filed with the Honorable Richard J. Oglesby, governor of the state of Illinois, on behalf of Giovanni Azari," no. 611, filed November 12, 1885, Illinois State Archives, Springfield, Illinois. But see "The Italian Murder," *Chicago Tribune*, June 24, 1885, 8 ("first order of business" was made in response to a motion objecting that the defendants had not been properly given the names of all the prospective jurors; after this was resolved Kane made her motions).

22. *Dacey*, 116 Ill. 555; Conley v. Illinois, 80 Ill. 236 (1875); Shirwin v. Illinois, 69 Ill. 55, 59 (1873) (rape case, judge ruling on continuance—in this case for three weeks, until the next term of court—should consider, inter alia, the nature of the charge); Austine v. Illinois, 110 Ill. 248 (1884) (defendant charged with assault and attempted rape, court should have granted the motion to continue the case until the next term, given the nature of the charge and the relevance of the evidence to be gathered to defendant's case).

23. Wray v. Illinois, 78 Ill. 212, 214 (1875) (due diligence requirement); Moody v. Illinois, 20 Ill. 315, 318-19 (1858) (materiality requirement); *Austine*, 110 Ill. at 253 (same). Cf. Gingrich v. Illinois, 34 Ill. 448, 456 (1864) (missing witness, with the Army of the Potomac in Virginia, was sick and behind enemy lines; court held an error to deny the motion for a continuance).

24. Schneir v. Illinois, 23 Ill. 17, 23-24 (1859); *Gardner*, 106 Ill. See also the discussion in two decisions that followed the verdict in this case. Chicago & Alton Railroad v. Shenk, 131 Ill. 283 (1890) (court held the failure to supply a competent interpreter an error), and Illinois v. Nitti, 312 Ill. 73, 89 (1924) (court noted the importance of providing translators in criminal cases).

25. *Schneir*, 23 Ill. at 23. Cf. Bartley v. Illinois, 156 Ill. 234 (1895).

26. *Logg*, 92 Ill. at 603 (reversible error to take contested issue of fact from the jury by means of an instruction); Collin v. Thomas, 13 Ill. App. 51, 53 (1883) (instruction contained a finding inconsistent with the evidence and on a contested question of fact); Pittsburgh, Cincinnati & St. Louis Railroad v. Gost, 13 Ill. App. 619 (1883) (instruction that prevented jury from considering the possibility of contributory negligence); Pittsburgh, Cincinnati & St. Louis Railroad v. McGrath, 15 Ill. App. 85, 89 (1884) (error to give an instruction that kept the jury from considering the implications of the fellow servant rule); Cole v. Cosgrove, 16 Ill. App. 167, 169 (1885) (error to give instruction that assumed all the defendants participated in a fraud, this was a question for the jury to decide).

27. Griffin v. Illinois, 351 U.S. 12, 18 (1956). By the time Griffin and his codefendant were tried, Illinois law had become slightly less harsh, and indigent defendants convicted of capital crimes were entitled to a free trial transcript. This would actually have protected the defendants in the Trunk Murder case, as would another recent rule in Illinois, Illinois Supreme Court Rule 323c, which provides that a "bystanders report"—or summary of proceedings based on the "best available sources, including recollection"—may be substituted for a trial transcript. For the rule in the 1880s, see *Illinois Revised Statutes*, ch. 33 §5; Ingraham v. People, 94 Ill. 428, 429 (1880); and the correspondence in "Application for a reprieve filed on behalf of Frank Mulkowski, on December 26, 1885," no. 640 1/2, Springfield, Illinois.

28. "Notes," *American Law Review* 18 (1884): 451, 487. See also Dale, *"People v. Coughlin,"* 534.

29. Currey, *Chicago*, 4:264; "The Psychology of Murder," *International Review* 3 (January 1876): 73; *Addresses Delivered by John A. Taylor in the Cases of Burroughs and Fuchs Who Were Indicted and Tried for Murder* (New York, 1882), 21 (urging that insanity

be defined by common sense); *Proceedings in the Second Trial in* United States v. John W. Dorsey et al. (Washington, D.C., 1883), 1577 (common sense should guide determination of what evidence should go to the jury); John T. Stuart et al., *The Trial of Daniel Clever, Indicted for Murder* (Carlisle, Pa., 1885) ("common sense and mankind" say it is just for a man to kill another man whom he believed to be committing adultery with his wife). See also Pfeifer, *Rough Justice*, 105 (in the 1890s C. W. Bramel, a judge in Wyoming, embraced communal [that is, commonsense] notions of justice and ignored the requirements of due process).

30. "Notes," *American Law Review* 18 (1884): 487–88. For a later criticism of the practice, see Roscoe Pound, "Law in Books and Law in Action," *American Law Review* 44 (1910): 12, 18.

31. Pound, "Law in Books," 12, 18–19; "He Realizes the Danger," *Chicago Times*, January 21, 1889, 1–2 (criticisms of the criminal justice system in Chicago); Ferrari, "New York County Criminal Courts," 194 (immigrant defendants in New York City). See also Elizabeth Dale, "Criminal Justice in the United States, 1790–1920: A Government of Laws or Men?" in *Cambridge History of Law in America*, ed. Christopher Tomlins and Michael Grossberg (New York: Cambridge University Press, 2008), 2:133; Clare V. McKanna, *The Trial of "Indian Joe": Race and Justice in the Nineteenth-Century West* (Lincoln: University of Nebraska Press, 2003).

Conclusion

1. "Editorial," *Chicago Times*, June 29, 1885, 4 (quote); "Three at Once," *Chicago Times*, November 15, 1885, 13.

Appendix A

1. The Italian vital records, which record birth, death, baptism, and marriage, are known as the *Registri dello stato civile* and were maintained by the Ufficio dello Stato Civile. The records for Termini Imerese (*Registri dello stato civile di Termini Imerese* [Palermo], 1820–1910) and Trabia (*Registri dello stato civile di Trabia* [Palermo], 1820–1910) have been collected by the Church of the Latter Day Saints (LDS) and are available in microfilm at their archives. Some of the information from those films has also been entered in an online database maintained by the LDS at www.familysearch.org. The vital records from Termini Imerese are being transcribed into English records that are available online (there is a membership fee) at the Termini Imerese database at www.terminiimerese.org.

Passenger lists are available on microfilm in the *Passenger and Crew Lists of Vessels Arriving at New York, New York*, National Archives Microfilm Publications, M237. Some of these records have been transcribed in *Italians to America: Lists of Passengers Arriving at U.S. Ports, 1880–1899*, ed. Ira A. Glazier and P. William Filby (Wilmington, Del.: Scholarly Resources, 1992). A searchable database derived from these records is available online (for a fee) at www.ancestry.com.

Bibliography

Primary Sources

Newspapers and Periodicals

Atlanta Constitution
Bangor Daily Whig & Courier (Maine)
Boston Daily
Boston Daily Advertiser
Chicago Daily News
Chicago Herald
Chicago Times
Chicago Tribune
Christian Science Monitor
Daily Arkansas Gazette (Little Rock)
Daily Graphic (New York City)
Daily Inter-Ocean (Chicago)
Milwaukee Daily Journal
Milwaukee Daily Sentinel
The Nation
New York Times
North American
Pittsburg Dispatch
St. Louis Globe-Democrat
Washington Post

Case Files, Reported Decisions, Statutes, and Constitutional Provisions

Andrews v. Illinois, 117 Ill. 195 (1886).
"Application for a pardon filed with the Honorable Richard J. Oglesby, governor of the state of Illinois, on behalf of Giovanni Azari." No. 611, filed November 12, 1885. Illinois State Archives, Springfield, Illinois.
"Application for a reprieve filed on behalf of Frank Mulkowski, on December 26, 1885." No. 640 1/2. Illinois State Archives, Springfield, Illinois.
Austine v. Illinois, 110 Ill. 248 (1884).
Bartley v. Illinois, 156 Ill. 234 (1895).
Blemer v. Illinois, 76 Ill. 265 (1875).

Blevings v. Illinois, 2 Ill. (1 Scam.) 171 (1835).

Chicago & Alton Railroad v. Shenk, 131 Ill. 283 (1890).

Cole v. Cosgrove, 16 Ill. App.167 (1885).

Collin v. Thomas, 13 Ill. App. 51 (1883).

Collins v. Illinois, 98 Ill. 584 (1881).

Conley v. Illinois, 80 Ill. 236 (1875).

Cross v. Illinois, 47 Ill. 152 (1868).

Fielden v. Illinois, 128 Ill. 595 (1890).

Foran Act. 23 Stat. 332 (1885).

Gardner v. Illinois, 106 Ill. 76 (1883).

Gates v. Illinois, 14 Ill. 433 (1853).

Gillespie v. Illinois, 176 Ill. 238 (1898).

Gingrich v. Illinois, 34 Ill. 448 (1864).

Griffin v. Illinois, 351 U.S. 12, 18 (1956).

Holliday v. Illinois, 10 Ill. 214 (1848).

Illinois Constitution. 1818, 1848, 1870.

Illinois Revised Statutes. Chapters 38, 65.

Illinois Supreme Court Rules.

Illinois v. Dacey, 116 Ill. 555 (1884).

Illinois v. Gates, 14 Ill. 433 (1853).

Illinois v. Nitti, 312 Ill. 73 (1924).

Ingraham v. People, 94 Ill. 428, 429 (1880).

Johnson v. Illinois, 22 Ill. 314 (1959).

Johnson v. Whiteside County, 110 Ill. 22 (1884).

Judiciary Act of 1793. 1 Stat. 333 (1793).

Kentucky v. Dennison, 65 U.S. 66 (1860).

Livar v. Texas, 26 Tex. Ct. App. 115 (1888).

Logg v. Illinois, 92 Ill. 598 (1879).

Louisiana v. Arbuno, 105 La. 719 (1900).

Lyons v. Illinois, 137 Ill. 602 (1891).

Marzen v. Illinois, 173 Ill. 43 (1898).

May v. Illinois, 92 Ill. 343 (1879).

Moody v. Illinois, 20 Ill. 315 (1858).

"Petition of John W. Bryam, attorney for the defendant, dated January 11, 1886, filed with Governor Richard J. Oglesby." People v. Mulkowski. Illinois State Archives, Springfield, Illinois.

"Petition of Kathryn Kane, attorney for the defendant, filed with Governor Richard J. Oglesby." People v. Silvestri et al. Illinois State Archives, Springfield, Illinois.

Pittsburgh, Cincinnati & St. Louis Railroad v. Gost, 13 Ill. App. 619 (1883).

Pittsburgh, Cincinnati & St. Louis Railroad v. McGrath, 15 Ill. App. 85 (1884).

Reynolds v. Illinois, 83 Ill 479 (1976).

Schneir v. Illinois, 23 Ill. 17 (1859).

Shirwin v. Illinois, 69 Ill. 55 (1873).

Slomer v. Illinois, 25 Ill. 70 (1860).

Spiegel's House Furnishing Co. v. Industrial Board of Illinois, 284 Ill. 90 (1918).

State of Illinois v. Ignazio Silvestri, et al., Term no. 1293, no 17521, Criminal Court of Cook County, Archives, Cook County, Richard J. Daley Center, Chicago, Illinois.

Sterling Brothers Co. v. Pearl, 80 Ill. 251 (1875).

United States Life Insurance Co. v. Vocke, 129 Ill. 557 (1889).
United States v. Marchant et al., 23 U.S. 480 (1827).
Vise v. County of Hamilton, 19 Ill. 78 (1857).
White v. Illinois, 81 Ill. 333 (1876).
Wray v. Illinois, 78 Ill. 212 (1875).

Published Trial Reports

The Allen Trials. New York, 1857.
Case of Colonel Dixon S. Miles. Washington, D.C., 1861.
Case of Monhaupt v. Central Park, North & East River Railroad. New York, 1883.
In the Matter of the Last Will and Testament of Patrick Dickie. New York, 1881.
The Italian Padrone Case: Trial of Antonio Giovanni Ancarola. New York, 1880.
Life and Confession of Charles Steingraver. Ashland, Ohio, 1852.
Red Nosed Mike! Wilkes-Barre, Pa., 1889.
Trial and Imprisonment of Geo. W. Felts. Rockford, Ill., 1907.
Trial of Francisco Gené Salvador. New York, 1866.
Trial of Impeachment of Patrick H. Laverty. Trenton, N.J., 1886.
Trial of John H. Reickles. South Carolina, 1858.
Trial of John H. Surratt. Washington D.C., 1867.
Trial of John J. Corcoran. New York, 1881.
Trial of Michael Cancemi. New York, 1858.
Trial of Michael J. Healy and Thomas J. Moran. Chicago, 1895.
Trial of Sarah Jane Robinson. Boston, 1888.
Trial of United States v. Ancarola. New York, 1880.

Studies and Government Reports

Chicago Civil Service Commission. *Final Report, Police Investigation.* Chicago, 1912.
Citizens' Police Committee. *Chicago Police Problems.* Chicago: University of Chicago Press, 1931.
Commissioner of Labor. *The Italians in Chicago: A Social and Economic Study.* Washington, D.C., 1897.
Illinois General Assembly. *Senate Report on the Chicago Police System.* Springfield, Ill.: Phillips Bros., 1898.
Koren, John. "The *Padrone* System and the *Padrone* Bank." *Bulletin of the Department of Labor* 9 (1897): 113, 135–39.
Manuscript Census for the United States, Chicago, Cook County, Illinois. 1880.
National Commission on Law Observance and Enforcement (the Wickersham Commission). *Report on Lawlessness in Law Enforcement.* Washington, D.C.: Government Printing Office, 1931.

Articles

"Confessions as Evidence of Guilt?" *Albany Law Journal* 11 (1875): 7.
"Current Topics." *Albany Law Journal* 10 (1874–1875): 98.
de Leveleye, Emile. "Pessimism on the Stage." *Eclectic Magazine of Foreign Literature* 42 (1885): 537.

Ferrari, Robert. "The Immigrant in the New York County Criminal Courts." *Journal of the American Institute of Criminal Law and Criminology* 3 (1912): 194, 202, 204, 207.

"The Psychology of Murder." *International Review* 3 (1876): 73, 88–90.

"Review: *La Criminologie*." *Juridical Review* 3 (1891): 161.

"Review: *The Criminal* by Havelock Ellis." *Juridical Review* 2 (1890): 381.

Seton, Citali. "The Secret Societies of Southern Italy: The Camorra, Feudalism and Brigandage, the Mafia." *Lippincott's Magazine of Popular Literature and Science* 143 (1879): 579, 590–92.

Sperenza, Gino C. "How It Feels to Be a Problem." *Charities* 22 (1904): 457.

——. "Lombroso in Science and Fiction." *Green Bag* 13 (1901): 122.

Wayland, H. L. "Social Science in the Laws of Moses: Wages and Pledges, Dignity of Labor, Crime, Humanity." *Journal of Social Sciences* 23 (1883): 167.

Zimmers, Helen. "Criminal Anthropology in Italy." *Green Bag* 10 (1898): 382.

Books and Pamphlets

Altgeld, John P. *The Chicago Martyrs: Reasons for Pardoning Fielden, Neebe and Schwab.* 1899.

Bench and Bar of Chicago: Biographical Sketches. Chicago, 1883.

Blackstone, William. *Commentaries on the Laws of England.* Vol. 4. 1769.

Bowen, Louise de Koven. *The Colored People of Chicago.* Chicago: Juvenile Prevention Association, 1913.

Brace, Charles Loring. *The Dangerous Classes of New York and Twenty Years among Them.* New York, 1872.

Cameron, Ossian. *Illinois Criminal Law and Practice.* Chicago, 1898.

Currey, J. Seymour. *Chicago, Its History and Its Builders: A Century of Marvelous Growth.* Vol. 4. Chicago, 1912.

Dugdale, Richard. *The Jukes: A Study in Crime, Pauperism, Disease and Heredity.* New York, 1877.

Franchetti, Leopoldo. *Condizioni politiche e amministrative della Sicilia.* 1876. Reprint, Rome: Donizelli, 2000.

Glazier, Ira. A., and P. William Filby, eds. *Italians to America: Lists of Passengers Arriving at U.S. Ports, 1880–1899.* Vols. 1–2. Wilmington, Del.: Scholarly Resources, 1992–.

Harris, I. C., comp. *Colored Men's Professional and Business Directory of Chicago.* Chicago: I. C. Harris, 1886.

Lakeside Annual Business Directory of the City of Chicago. Chicago: The Directory Company, 1885.

Lombroso, Cesare. *L'Uomo delinquente.* Torino, 1896–1897.

Munroe, Kirk. *The Murder of the Geogles and the Lynching of the Fiend Snyder.* Philadelphia, 1881.

Nuovo dizionario siciliano–italiano. Edited by Vincenzo Martillaro. 3rd ed. 1881. Reprint, Sala Bolognese: A Forini, 1997.

Romano, Santi. *L'ordinamento giuridico.* 1918. Reprint, Firenze: Sansoni, 1967.

Schaack, Michael. *Anarchy and Anarchists.* Chicago, 1889.

Smith, Josiah William. *A Manual of Common Law.* 1st American edition. Washington City, 1871.

Taylor, Alfred Swaine. *A Manual of Medical Jurisprudence.* 11th ed. Philadelphia: Lea Brothers, 1892.

Thompson, Seymour Dwight. *A Treatise on the Laws of Trials in Actions Civil and Criminal.* Chicago, 1889. Vol. 1, 38–39.

Vickers, Robert H. *The Powers and Duties of Police Officers and Coroners.* Chicago, 1889.

Wharton, Francis. *A Treatise on Criminal Pleading and Practice.* 8th ed. Philadelphia: Kay and Brother, 1880.

Secondary Sources

Theses and Dissertations

Eastwood, Cynthia. "A Study of the Regulations of Chicago Street Vendors." Ph.D. dissertation, University of Illinois, Chicago, 1988.

Harman, Kristyn Evelyn. "Aboriginal Convicts: Race, Law and Transportation in Colonial New South Wales." Ph.D. dissertation, University of Tasmania, 2008.

Iorizzo, Luciano John. "Italian Immigrants and the Impact of the *Padrone* System." Ph.D. dissertation, Syracuse University, 1966.

Jensen, Chris. "A Study of Lynching in Late Nineteenth Century Pennsylvania." B.A. honors thesis, Department of History, University of Florida, 2004.

Paxson, Gloria de la Garza. "The El Paso County Criminal Courts and Mexican-American Defendants: Unequal Justice during the 1920s." M.A. thesis, University of Texas, El Paso, 2003.

Vecoli, Rudolph John. "Chicago's Italians prior to World War I: A Study of Their Social and Economic Adjustment." Ph.D. dissertation, University of Wisconsin, 1963.

Articles

Abbott, Grace. "The Treatment of Aliens in the Criminal Court." *Journal of the American Institute of Criminal Law & Criminology* 2 (1912): 554, 558, 560–61.

Adler, Jeffrey. "'It Is His First Offense. We Might As Well Let Him Go': Homicide and Criminal Justice in Chicago, 1875–1920." *Journal of Social History* 40 (2006): 5–17.

Arredondo, Gabriela F. "Navigating Ethno-Racial Currents: Mexicans in Chicago, 1919–1939." *Journal of Urban History* 20 (2004): 399.

Bazelon, David L. "The Morality of the Criminal Law." *Southern California Law Review* 49 (1975–1976): 385, 400.

Bedau, Hugo Adam, and Michael L. Radelet. "Miscarriages of Justice in Potentially Capital Cases." *Stanford Law Review* 40 (1987): 21.

Bobiant, Anna di. "Genealogy of Soft Law." *American Journal of Comparative Law* 54 (2006): 499.

Boinson, Cara W. "Representing 'Miss Lizzie': Cultural Conviction in the Trial of Lizzie Borden." *Yale Journal of Law and the Humanities* 8 (1996): 351.

Bradwell, James H. "The Colored Bar in Chicago." *Michigan Law Review* 5 (1896): 385, 390.

Cohen, Thomas V. "Three Forms of Jeopardy: Honor, Pain, and Truth-Telling in a Sixteenth-Century Italian Courtroom." *Sixteenth Century Journal* 29 (1998): 975.

Colburn, David R., and George E. Pozzetta. "Crime and Ethnic Minorities in America: A Bibliographic Essay." *History Teacher* 7 (1974): 597.

Conley, Carolyn A. "Wars among Savages: Homicide and Ethnicity in the Victorian United Kingdom." *Journal of British Studies* 44 (2005): 775.

Crawford, Richard W. "The White Man's Justice: Native Americans and the Judicial System of San Diego County, 1870–1890." *Western Legal History* 5 (1992): 69.

D'Agostino, Peter. "Craniums, Criminals and the 'Cursed Race': Italian Anthropology in American Racial Thought, 1861–1924." *Comparative Studies in History and Society* 44 (2002): 319.

Dale, Elizabeth. "Criminal Justice in the United States, 1790–1920: A Government of Laws or Men?" In *Cambridge History of Law in America*, ed. Christopher Tomlins and Michael Grossberg, 2:133. New York: Cambridge University Press, 2008.

———. "A Different Sort of Justice: The Informal Courts of Public Opinion in Antebellum South Carolina." *South Carolina Law Review* 54 (2003): 627.

———. "It Makes Nothing Happen: Reasons for Studying the History of Law." *Law, Culture and the Humanities* 5 (2009): 3.

———. "Not Simply Black and White: Jury Power in the Late Nineteenth Century." *Social Science History* 25 (2001): 7.

———. "*People v. Coughlin* and Criticisms of the Criminal Jury in Late Nineteenth-Century Chicago." *Northern Illinois University Law Review* 28 (2008): 503, 515, 534.

———. "Popular Sovereignty: A Case Study from the Antebellum Era." In *Constitutional Mythologies: New Perspectives on Controlling the State*, ed. Alain Marciano. New York: Springer, forthcoming.

———. "'Social Equality Does Not Exist among Themselves, nor among Us': *Baylies v. Curry* and Civil Rights in Chicago, 1888." *American Historical Review* 107 (1997): 311.

Darnton, Robert. "It Happened One Night." *New York Review of Books* 51 (June 24, 2004): 60, 63–64.

Day, Jared N. "Credit, Capital, and Community: Informal Banking in Immigrant Communities in the United States, 1880–1924." *Financial History Review* (2002): 65, 72.

Drizin, Steven A., and Marissa J. Reich. "Heeding the Lessons of History: The Need for Mandatory Recording of Police Interrogation to Accurately Assess the Reliability and Voluntariness of Confessions." *Drake Law Review* 52 (2004): 619.

Fineschi, V., A. S. Dell'Erba, M. D. Paolo, and P. Pocaccianti. "Typical Homicide Ritual of the Italian Mafia (Incaprettamento)." *American Journal of Medical Pathology* 19 (1998): 87.

Fisher, William III. "Texts and Contexts: The Application to American Legal History of the Methodologies of Intellectual History." *Stanford Law Review* 49 (1997): 1065, 1070–74.

Garcia, Mario T. "Profirian Diplomacy and the Administration of Justice in Texas, 1877–1900." *Aztlan* 16 (1985): 1.

Gibson, Campbell J., and Emily Lennon. "Historical Census Statistics on the Foreign-born Population of the United States: 1850–1990." U.S. Census Bureau, Population Division, February 1991. www.census.gov/population/www/documentation/twps0029/twps0029.html/.

Gunther, Vanessa. "Indians and the Criminal Justice System in San Bernardino and San Diego Counties, 1850–1900." *Journal of the West* 39 (2000): 26.

Hiettler, Paul T. "A Surprising Amount of Justice: The Experience of Mexican and Racial Minority Defendants Charged with Serious Crimes in Arizona, 1865–1920." *Pacific Historical Review* 70 (2001): 193.

Hoverkamp, Herbert. "Evolutionary Models in Jurisprudence." *Texas Law Review* 64 (1985): 645.

Joens, David A. "John W. E. Thomas and the Election of the First African American to the Illinois General Assembly." *Journal of the Illinois Historical Society* 94 (2001): 200.

Kassim, Saul M. "The Psychology of Confessions." *Annual Review of Law and Social Science* 4 (2008): 193–95, 201–2.

Lammers, John C. "The Accommodation of Chinese Immigrants in Early California Courts." *Sociological Perspectives* 31 (1988): 446.

Miller, Batya. "Enforcement of the Sunday Closing Laws on the Lower East Side, 1820–1903." *American Jewish History* 91 (2003): 269.

Muhammad, Khalil G. "Race, Crime, and Social Mobility: Black and Italian Undesirables in Modern America." *Proceedings of the American Italian Historical Association* 30 (1997): 172.

Munn, Christopher. "The Transportation of Chinese Convicts from Hong Kong, 1844–1858." *Journal of the Canadian Historical Association* 8 (1997): 113.

Nelli, Humbert S. "Italians and Crime in Chicago: The Formative Years, 1890–1920." *American Journal of Sociology* 74 (1969): 373.

———. "The *Padrone* System: An Exchange of Letters." *Labor History* 17 (1976): 406.

Osofsky, Gilbert. "Race Riot, 1900: A Study of Ethnic Violence." *Journal of Negro Education* 32 (1964): 16.

Page, Clemson N., Jr. "A Legacy of an Age." *Pennsylvania Lawyers* 23 (2001): 34.

Parker, Linda S. "Statutory Changes and Ethnicity in Sex Crimes in our California Counties, 1880–1920." *Western Legal History* 6 (1993): 69.

Peck, Gunther. "Reinventing Free Labor: Immigrant Padrones and Contract Laborers in North America, 1885–1925." *Journal of American History* 83 (1996): 848, 850–51.

Pound, Roscoe. "Law in Books and Law in Action." *American Law Review* 44 (1910): 12, 18–19.

Rafter, Nicole Hahn. "Seeing and Believing: Images of Heredity in Biological Theories of Crime." *Brooklyn Law Review* 6 (2001): 71.

Riall, Lucy. "Elites in Search of Authority: Political Power and Social Order in Nineteenth-Century Sicily." *History Workshop Journal* 55 (2003): 25.

———. "Garibaldi and the South." In *Italy in the Nineteenth Century, 1796–1900*, ed. John A. Davis, 132–53. Oxford: Oxford University Press, 2000.

Robinson, Leila J. "Women Lawyers in the United States." *Green Bag* 2 (1890): 10.

Snodgrass, J. William. "The Black Press in the San Francisco Bay Area, 1856–1900." *California History* 60 (1981–1982): 306.

Soresina, Marco. "Pietro Ellero and the Debate on the Death Penalty, 1861–1865." *Risorgimento* 38 (1986): 96.

Spitzzeri, Paul R. "On a Case-by-Case Basis: Ethnicity and Los Angeles Courts, 1850–1870." *California History* 83 (2005): 26.

Tanenhaus, David, and Steven A. Drizin. "'Owing to the Extreme Youth of the Accused': The Chicago Legal Response to Juvenile Homicide." *Journal of Criminal Law and Criminology* 92 (2001–2002): 641.

Todd, Jesse T., Jr. "Battling Satan in the City: Charles Henry Parkhurst and Municipal Redemption in Gilded Age New York." *American Presbyterian* 71 (1993): 243.

Trotti, Michael A. "The Lure of the Sensational Murder." *Journal of Social History* 35 (2001): 429.

Vaughn, H. H. "The Implications of Dialect in Italy." *Italica* 3 (1928): 56.

———. "Studies in Italian Linguistics." *Italica* 13 (1936): 74, 78.

Watts, Eugene J. "The Police in Atlanta." *Journal of Southern History* 39 (1973): 165.

West, Elliott. "Cleansing the Queen City: Prohibition and Urban Reform in Denver." *Arizona and the West* 14 (1972): 331.

Willrich, Michael. "Criminal Justice in the United States." In *Cambridge History of Law in America: The Twentieth Century and After*, ed. Christopher Tomlins and Michael Grossberg, vol. 3, 195. New York: Cambridge University Press, 2008.

Wong, K. Scott. "'The Eagle Seeks a Helpless Quarry': Chinatown, the Police, and the Press." *Amerasia Journal* 22 (1996): 81.

Wright, George C. "The Billy Club and the Ballot: Police Intimidation of Blacks in Louisville, Kentucky, 1880–1930." *Southern Studies* 23 (1994): 20.

Books

Adler, Jeffrey. *First in Violence, Deepest in Dirt: Homicide in Chicago, 1875–1920.* Cambridge: Harvard University Press, 2006.

Auerbach, Sascha. *Race, Law, and "The Chinese Puzzle" in Imperial Britain.* New York: Palgrave MacMillan, 2009.

Avrich, Paul. *The Haymarket Tragedy.* Princeton: Princeton University Press, 1984.

Banfield, Edward C. *The Moral Basis of a Backward Society.* New York: Free Press, 1967.

Banner, Stuart. *The Death Penalty: An American History.* Cambridge: Harvard University Press, 2002.

Bederman, Gail. *Manliness and Civilization: A Cultural History of Gender and Race in the United States, 1880–1917.* Chicago: University of Chicago Press, 1995.

Bench and Bar in Chicago: Biographical Sketches. Chicago: American Biographical Publishing Company, 1883.

Blok, Anton. *The Mafia of a Sicilian Village: A Study of Violent Peasant Entrepreneurs.* New York: Waveland Press, 1974.

Brundage, W. Fitzhugh. *Lynching in the New South: Georgia and Virginia, 1880–1930.* Urbana: University of Illinois Press, 1993.

Colin, Joan, and Ruth Morris. *Interpreters and the Legal Process.* Winchester, U.K.: Waterside Press, 1996.

Currey, Josiah Seymour. *Chicago, Its History and Its Builders: A Century of Marvellous Growth.* Chicago: S. J. Clarke Publishing, 1912. Vol. 4.

Dale, Elizabeth. *The Rule of Justice: The People of Chicago versus Zephyr Davis.* Columbus: Ohio State University Press, 2001.

Davis, John A., ed. *Italy in the Nineteenth Century, 1796–1900.* Oxford: Oxford University Press, 2000.

Dickie, John. *Cosa Nostra: A History of the Sicilian Mafia.* London: Hodder and Stoughton, 2004.

DiMaio, Vincent J. M., and Suzanna E. Dana. *Handbook of Forensic Pathology.* Austin: Landes Bioscience, 1998.

Duis, Perry R. *Challenging Chicago: Coping with Everyday Life, 1837–1920.* Urbana: University of Illinois Press, 1998.

Edwards, Laura F. *The People and Their Peace: Legal Culture and the Transformation of Inequality in the Post-revolutionary South.* Chapel Hill: University of North Carolina Press, 2009.

Flinn, John Joseph, and John Elbert Wilkie. *A History of the Chicago Police.* 1887. Chicago: Police Book Fund; reprint, New York: AMS Press, 1973.

Friedman, Lawrence M. *American Law in the Twentieth Century.* New Haven: Yale University Press, 2002.

———. *Crime and Punishment in American History.* New York: Basic Books, 1993.

———. *A History of American Law.* 3rd ed. New York: Touchstone, 2005.

Gambetta, Diego. *The Sicilian Mafia: The Business of Private Protection.* Cambridge: Harvard University Press, 1993.

Gambino, Richard. *Vendetta.* Garden City: Doubleday, 1977.

Gibson, Mary. *Born to Crime: Cesare Lombroso and the Origins of Biological Criminality.* Westport, Conn.: Praeger, 2002.

Green, James R. *Death in the Haymarket: A Story of Chicago, the First Labor Movement, and the Bombing that Divided Gilded Age America.* New York: Pantheon Books, 2006.

Grossman, James R., Ann Durkin Keating, and Janice L. Reiff, eds. *The Encyclopedia of*

Chicago. Chicago: University of Chicago Press, 2004. Available online at www.encyclopedia.chicagohistory.org/.

Ledgeway, Adam. *A Comparative Syntax of the Dialects of Southern Italy: A Minimalist Approach.* Oxford: Blackwell, 2000.

Lindberg, Richard. *To Serve and Collect: Chicago Politics and Police Corruption from the Lager Beer Riot to the Summerdale Scandal.* New York: Praeger. 1991.

Lui, Mary Ting Yi. *The Chinatown Trunk Mystery: Murder, Miscegenation, and Other Dangerous Encounters in Turn-of-the-Century New York City.* Princeton: Princeton University Press, 2005.

McKanna. Clare V. *The Trial of "Indian Joe": Race and Justice in the Nineteenth-Century West.* Lincoln: University of Nebraska Press, 2003.

McNamee, Gwen Hoerr, ed. *Bar None: 125 Years of Women Lawyers in Illinois.* Chicago: Chicago Bar Association Alliance for Women, 1998.

Moe, Nelson. *The View from Vesuvius: Italian Culture and the Southern Question.* Berkeley and Los Angeles: University of California Press, 2002.

Monkkonen, Eric. *Police in Urban America, 1860–1920.* New York: Cambridge University Press, 2004.

Nelli, Humbert S. *Italians in Chicago, 1880–1930: A Study in Ethnic Mobility.* New York: Oxford University Press, 1970.

Novak, William J. *The People's Welfare: Law and Regulation in Nineteenth-Century America.* Chapel Hill: University of North Carolina Press, 1996.

Pfeifer, Michael J. *Rough Justice: Lynching and American Society, 1874–1947.* Urbana: University of Illinois Press, 2004.

Privitera, Joseph Frederic. *Basic Sicilian: A Brief Reference Grammar.* New York: Mellen Press, 1998.

Putnam, Robert D. *Making Democracy Work: Civic Traditions in Modern Italy.* Princeton: Princeton University Press, 1994.

Reed, Christopher Robert. *Black Chicago's First Century, 1883–1900.* Columbia: University of Missouri Press, 2005.

Sachs, Jessica Snyder. *Corpse: Nature, Forensics, and the Struggle to Pinpoint Time of Death.* New York: Basic Books, 2002.

Salvatore, Nick. *Eugene V. Debs: Citizen and Socialist.* Urbana: University of Illinois Press, 1982.

Schneider, Jane, ed. *Italy's "Southern Question": Orientalism in One Country.* New York: Berg, 1997.

Schneider, Jane C., and Peter T. Schneider. *Reversible Destiny: Mafia, Anti-Mafia, and the Struggle for Palermo.* Berkeley and Los Angeles: University of California Press, 2003.

Schneirov, Richard. *Labor and Urban Politics: Class Conflict and the Origins of Modern Liberalism in Chicago, 1864–1897.* Urbana: University of Illinois Press, 1998.

Sloat, Warren. *A Battle for the Soul of New York: Tammany Hall, Police Corruption, Vice and the Reverend Charles Parkurst's Crusade against Them, 1892–1895.* New York: Copper Square, 2002.

Smith, Carl. *Urban Disorder and the Shape of Disbelief: The Great Chicago Fire, the Haymarket Bomb, and the Model Town of Pullman.* 2nd ed. Chicago: University of Chicago Press, 2007.

Smith, J. Clay. *Emancipation: The Making of the Black Lawyer, 1844–1944.* Philadelphia: University of Pennsylvania Press, 1993.

Stille, Alexander. *Excellent Cadavers: The Mafia and the Death of the First Italian Republic.* New York: Vintage Press, 1996.

Tanenhaus, David. *Juvenile Justice in the Making*. New York: Oxford University Press, 2004.

Waldrep, Christopher. *Roots of Disorder: Race and Criminal Justice in the American South*. Urbana: University of Illinois Press, 1998.

Wells, Tom, and Richard A. Leo. *The Wrong Guys: Murder, False Confessions, and the Norfolk Four*. New York: New Press, 2008.

Willrich, Michael. *City of Courts: Socializing Justice in Progressive Era Chicago*. New York: Cambridge University Press, 2003.

Zimring, Franklin E. *American Capital Punishment*. New York: Oxford University Press, 2004.

Index